WESTMINSTER CATHEDRAL:

FROM DREAM TO REALITY

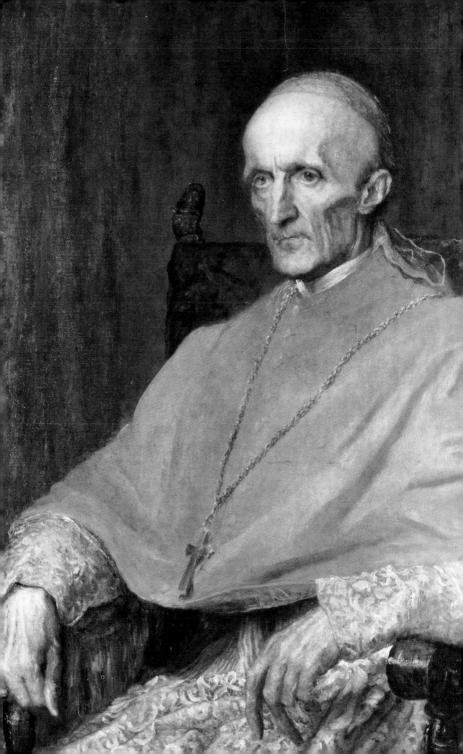

WESTMINSTER CATHEDRAL:

From Dream to Reality

Rene Kollar

Faith & Life Publications Ltd
Edinburgh

F & L Publications Ltd
The Easter Experience
173 Easter Road
Edinburgh   EH6 8LF
Scotland

British Library Cataloguing-in-Publication Data available

Frontispiece: His Emminence Cardinal H E Manning, by courtesy of the National Portrait Gallery

ISBN 0 948095 25 3

Printed by Swannack Brown & Co. Ltd., Hull, England.

CONTENTS

List of Illustrations

FOREWORD

Here is a book by an American scholar who has got hold of a remarkable but previously hidden story and who tells it concisely and well. This is the story behind the building of the Cathedral which is, more than any other church, the symbol of Roman Catholicism in England. In particular it is the mother church of a diocese covering London north of the Thames and the surrounding counties. But here am I, an Englishman who serves in the Anglican Cathedral on the south bank of the river. The Thames has often been thought to be as divisive as the Atlantic itself, as unbridgeable as the historic gulf between Catholic and Protestant!

Yet in a few ways I feel qualified to comment on this book. For one thing, I love reading (and even trying to write) church history when it is human and honest. These are characteristics of Professor Kollar's study. He tells of tensions between monks and parish priests and between the English and the French Benedictines, frustrating the first plans of a strangely clumsy cardinal - plans which would have created a Benedictine abbey in the heart of London. But I also love worship in a Cathedral. I knew Westminster Cathedral from the inside when I was a neighbour as a Canon of Westminster Abbey. Now, when I drop in, I am hit - a better word would be embraced - by the atmosphere of prayer, with or without the famous music and the large congregations. And so this is a story of ecumenical and enduring significance, for it is the story of a determination to establish the worship of God so splendidly that the liturgy would match Bentley's architecture, with teaching and pastoral care that would touch the hearts and lives of a great multitude. The problems and the disputes make good reading. But Cardinal Vaughan's dream which came true is what really matters, and it fortifies the soul.

It was a triumphalist dream. Roman Catholicism had emerged from the persecution of the Recusants and the poverty of the Irish immigrants. It wanted to say so in a London which was then the capital not only of a prosperous industrial nation but also of an empire including a quarter of the human race. Today England is humbler – and so is Roman Catholicism. And that is spiritually healthier, by the standards of the New Testament; which is why I so admire the programme of the Cathedral's lively conference centre. But his story of a Cathedral soaring to heaven from beginnings full of the earth of human nature is perpetually encouraging, like the story of the ladder in Jacob's dream.

DAVID L EDWARDS
Southwark Cathedral
London SE1

PREFACE
by the Right Reverand Francis Rossiter, OSB

This book, *Westminster Cathedral: from dream to reality*, is a scholarly account of Cardinal Vaughan's plans and negotiations to bring about a Benedictine liturgical presence in his cathedral. It bears the mark of the meticulous scholarship of the author, Dom Rene Kollar OSB, of St. Vincent's Archabbey, Latrobe, Pennsylvania, whose researches into the early history of Ealing Abbey also led him to the beginnings of Westminster Cathedral. This fascinating study will be of great interest, not only to Benedictines, but also to all those people who love and cherish this great and important Roman Catholic Cathedral of Westminster.

Hindsight surely shows that Cardinal Vaughan's scheme to approach both the English and the French Benedictines to perform the liturgy in his cathedral was an extraordinary one. The author shows how very suspicious the English and French were of each other in the days before the *entente cordiale*, along with the understandably defensive stance adopted both by the English Benedictines and the English Roman Catholics. It is surprising that the Cardinal never realised how impractical his scheme really was.

The idea of a French monastery in Westminster, with either a French or a joint English/French Community being responsible for the liturgical life of the cathedral, was a strange one; as was his concept of the Ealing Community commuting daily to the cathedral for that purpose. The clear insights and the practical approach to the proposition by Cardinal Gasquet comes out well in the correspondence cited by Professor Kollar. Gasquet realised at an early stage that the proposals would not work.

But one is left admiring both the vision and determination of Cardinal Vaughan to establish a strong liturgical life within his cathedral, and his ultimate humble acceptance of the fact that this would best be done after all by priests of the archdiocese who were resident at the cathedral. History has confirmed his judgement, with people the world over enjoying its fruits. Professor Kollar's fascinating story fills a real gap, to our lasting benefit.

Publisher's note

We acknowledge with gratitude permission to use copyright material: the Frontispiece from the National Portrait Gallery; sundry archive material from Westminster Cathedral archives; similar use from the Mill Hill Fathers; Farnborough abbey, Downside abbey, Solesmes abbey, Ealing abbey and *The Universe*

INTRODUCTION

'The Roman Catholics after 1832,' according to Owen Chadwick, 'blinked like owls at the daylight and they came into the sun and found its rays benevolent and exciting.'[1] Fed by the Irish escaping the famine or searching for a new and better life, the membership of the Roman Church also grew. Native Britons who had clung to their faith became respectable, and the conversion to Rome of some prominent Anglicans helped to destroy the stereotype of English Roman Catholics being ignorant and superstitious foreigners. Yet, suspicions on the part of many English toward Roman Catholicism persisted. Although ignored in some cases, statute law against Roman Catholics had marked them as second class citizens. Catholic emancipation removed some political disabilities, but numerous other restrictions were enacted against them as part of that act to ensure its successful passage. Educational opportunities at the ancient universities were still closed to Catholics, and they were removed only with great difficulty. Guy Fawkes's, parades, anti-popery demonstrations, and organisations of loyal Protestants dedicated to opposing the dangers of popery still coloured the social and religious life of Victorian England. In spite of this, Roman Catholicism grew in strength and vitality.

However, Catholics in Britain still did not have their own hierarchy, which had been outlawed by the actions of Henry VIII and his Anglican successors. The Propaganda in Rome (a Committee of Cardinals directing foreign missions) directed the spiritual and temporal affairs of Catholics in Britain. In the eyes of the Vatican, it was a missionary territory or province, and the day-to-day administration of the Catholic Church was entrusted to the Vicars Apostolic. While not emancipated from Propaganda control until the next century, Victorian Catholic laymen, priests and even the Vicars Apostolic clamoured for the establishment of their own hierarchy. By 1850, the time seemed ripe.

Aware that a brief to establish bishops might cause trouble in England, Rome steadily insisted on three conditions for its promulgation. It must be done while a Whig government ruled England; must be published at a time of year when Parliament was not sitting; and must establish sees of which the titles did not transgress the emancipation act of 1829, and therefore avoided all titles used by bishops of the Church of England.[2]

The reaction to the Pope's decision to establish a Roman Catholic hierarchy demonstrated that a subtle but volatile stream of religious prejudice still thrived. Burnings in effigy, angry no-popery demonstrations, press reports which spelled out the lurid danger of 'papal aggression', and even a statute law, exposed the British fear and suspicion of this assertive Roman Catholic action. Russell's 'Durham Letter' and Nicholas Wiseman's 'Flaminian Gate' pastoral exhibited two opposing viewpoints. The Roman Catholics, however, must take some responsibility for the outbreaks of violence and vituperation. In the opinion of many, the timing and rhetoric of Rome was both an affront and a challenge to Anglican hegemony. The first Archbishop, N P S Wiseman (1802-1865), lacked the skills of the diplomat and appeared as an arrogant rival. Moreover, Rome's lack of sensitivity and appreciation of England's troubled religious history increased the tension. To the majority of Anglicans, the establishment of a Roman Catholic Archdiocese of Westminster was an insult: 'Propaganda was not sufficiently aware how hallowed to England was the name of Westminster.'[3]

Toward the end of the century, the memory and tradition associated with Westminster occasioned another religious controversy. But this time, it was some elements of the Roman Catholic community itself which became involved in a conflict which publicly challenged their proud claim of unity and homogeneity. The growth in membership necessitated an increase in the building of churches for Catholics, and these new places of worship became tangible reminders of the Roman Catholic claim to maturity and full membership in the religious community of Great Britain. Moreover, the idea of a grand cathedral which would rival anything in the established church had long been a dream of zealous Roman Catholics. It was not until Herbert Vaughan became Archbishop, in 1892, that this new Westminster showed any signs of success. Vaughan wanted to re-create the splendours of pre-Reformation England in the centre of the nations's capital. Monks were consequently needed, and Vaughan invited the Benedictine monks from Downside Abbey in Somerset to come to his new cathedral to chant the ancient Latin office.

As soon as his plan was revealed, the secular clergy of Vaughan's archdiocese resented the intrusion of these monks into what they believed was their exclusive domain. Almost immediately the old tension which had existed between religious and seculars (i.e. monks and priests) re-appeared in the press, and was vigorously debated in speeches, pamphlets and the minutes of the Cathedral Chapter. In the middle of this squabble, Cardinal Vaughan secretly contacted the French monks of Solesmes Abbey and invited them to take the place he had already promised to their English counterparts! When the English Benedictine Congregation was informed, their violent reaction shocked the naive Cardinal. It was their prerogative alone, these monks claimed, to sing the Divine Office in the new Westminster, and it must not be surrendered to a group of foreigners, albeit fellow Benedictines. The presence of French monks at Westminster would be unpatriotic, imprudent, an insult to all things English. To escape from this embarrassing situation, Vaughan was eventually forced to entrust the liturgy and choral services of Westminster to the Cathedral Chapter. The following pages tell the story of this abortive and unsuccessful attempt to establish a community of Benedictine monks at London's new Westminster Cathedral.

This book is a part of a larger study dealing with the Benedictine presence in London, which still exists today. The Abbot President of the English Benedictine Congregation, Francis Rossiter, and the monks of Ealing Abbey have supported and encouraged my research for several years. Miss Elizabeth Poyser at Archbishop's House has always extended kind advice and friendship. Rev Brice Ryan, O S B, Chairperson of Foreign Languages at St. Vincent College, freely shared his knowledge of French in the translations and culture and monastic history. St. Vincent Archabbey continues to be my chief inspiration, and the College has eased the problems of travel by two faculty development grants. John Elliott's optimism and dedication to Benedictine research is a constant inspiration.

I. CATHOLICISM IN ENGLAND FROM THE REFORMATION

The Henrician Reformation radically transformed the social and religious life of England, and for at least two centuries many stereotyped Roman Catholicism as a threat to the integrity and security of the realm. The Roman Catholic Church, however, had come under attack from many sources prior to the reign of Henry VIII; a desire to correct ecclesiastical abuses had been voiced before the Reformation Parliament assembled in 1529. The problem of church appointments to English posts by Roman officials and appeals to ecclesiastical courts in Rome had constantly plagued church-state relationships. During the fourteenth century, the Statutes of Praemunire and Provisors attempted to limit the pretentions of the Roman Church which had been growing since the time of Henry II. In the areas of theological speculation and ecclesiastical practice, some pious and brave individuals seriously questioned the accepted norms and interpretations provided by the Roman Church. With its emphasis on the importance of a direct and personal experience of God, mysticism turned the eyes of its followers heavenward and helped to undercut both the role of the priest as mediator and the claim of the institutional church as the exclusive dispensor of salvation. Some of the writings of the Oxford don, John Wycliffe (c. 1329-1384) anticipated many of the programmes advanced by the later reformers: the need for the bible in the vernacular; doubt concerning the doctrine of transubstantiation; the propriety of ecclesiastical ownership of property; the priority of sacred scripture; the need to reform the scandalously lax lives of monks and nuns; and questions concerning the superstitious character of relics, pilgrimages, and the cult of the saints.

Not surprisingly, ecclesiastical abuses and scandals attracted much attention. In *The Canterbury Tales*, for example, Geoffrey Chaucer's lively vignettes portrayed churchmen and churchwomen still strongly attached to the lures and enjoyments of the world which they had vowed to renounce. Another fourteenth century piece of literature, *Piers Plowman*, written by William Langland, castigated the wealth and extravagances of an institutional church dedicated to poverty. The humanists and students of the 'new learning' also recognised some of the shortcomings and hoped to correct them by poking fun through satire. Erasmus (c. 1469-1536), whose 'sensible and scholarly nose was otherwise offended by the stink of corruption', became one of the chief representatives of this school of thought. His works, especially *The Praise of Folly* and *The Colloquies*, captured a wide audience and exerted a great influence throughout Europe. 'More than any single man, he lowered the European reputation of popes and clergy, monks and friars, and (above all) of the theologians.'[2] At the dawn of the sixteenth century, therefore, the complaints and critiques against the Roman Catholic Church seemed innumerable and even insurmountable: the immoral or luxurious lifestyle of nuns and clerics; the benefit of clergy; sanctuary; mortuary fees; and the wide-reaching claims of the clerical courts. Reform was long overdue, and 'like Erasmus, many educated men would have preferred the Church to be ridiculed into good sense and efficiency and purity of life. 'But a man who is holding property will not be mocked out of it.'[3]

Unlike the reforming movements on the continent, the English Reformation was an act of state. The King

in Parliament reversed centuries of custom, tinkered with the liturgy and, of course, revolutionized the relationship of England to the Pope in Rome. Henry VIII had agonized over ways to save his kingdom from the chaos and upheavals associated with the War of the Roses, and a male heir became an urgent necessity to give stability to his dynasty. Moreover, Henry tried to resist radical changes in religious practices or in doctrine. Innovations in the area of religion could not remain isolated from the demands of political expediency.

Henry's Spanish queen, Catherine of Aragon, had grown old and sterile, and he had already cast fond eyes on Ann Boleyn, but the chances of a papal annulment seemed remote if not impossible – not least because Catherine's nephew, the Emperor Charles V, had sacked Rome and held the Pope under house arrest! Frustrated and eager to re-marry, Henry dismissed Cardinal Wolsey, who was unsuccessful in obtaining the necessary divorce from Rome and even failed in having the case heard in England, and summoned Parliament in 1529. So reform of the Roman Catholic Church commenced.

A series of statutes attacked the traditional privileges of the Church and transformed England into a unitary national state. The Convocations of Canterbury and York paid fines of approximately £118,000 for alleged violations of the *Statute of Praemunire*. In 1532, the *Act of Submission of the Clergy* prohibited enactment of any new ecclesiastical laws without royal permission, and the Church also agreed to submit the existing canons to a committee of laymen and clerics for review and possible revision. The economic aspects also crept into the legislation: annates or first fruits were no longer paid to Rome, but instead went to the Crown's coffers. The *Act in Restraint of Appeals* (1534) abolished appeals from England to Rome. Henry divorced his wife and married his mistress, Ann Boleyn, in 1533, and so Catherine was denied access to the ecclesiastical courts in Rome. More importantly, the *Act in Restraint of Appeals* also signalled the advent of a new national and independent state. According to the preamble,

> by divers sundry old authentic histories and chronicles it is manifestly declared and expressed, that this realm of England is an empire . . . governed by one supreme head and king . . . unto whom a body politic, composed of all sorts and degrees of people, divided in terms, and by names of spirituality and temporality, be bounden and august to bear, next to God, a natural and humble obedience.

Consequently, the *Act of Supremacy* (1534) declared that the king was now the supreme head of the Church of England. With the exceptions of Thomas More and John Fisher, acts of heroism and displays of loyalty to Roman Catholicism were rare. The momentum of reform continued, and monastic houses became the next victims of Henry's policies.

On the eve of the Reformation, approximately eight hundred religious houses of various sizes and wealth dotted the English countryside. For some time the monasteries had failed to contribute significantly to the religious or intellectual climate of England, but on the other hand they were not the dens of licentiousness and drunkeness which some critics claimed. Rather, they had grown complaisant, and the small number of monks was out of proportion to their vast wealth: ' . . . for the most part the monasteries were neither fervent nor disgraceful. They were pleasant, half-secularized clubs for common and comfortable living. Some of the smaller were little more than farms.'[4] The monasteries caught the keen eye of Henry VIII for two reasons: their wealth would greatly enrich the royal purse; and, as enclaves of loyal Roman Catholics, they might easily become seedbeds of sedition. Consequently, the monasteries must be suppressed and their extensive lands become royal property.

The first hint of a national policy had already appeared between 1524 and 1529, when Cardinal Wolsey suppressed a number of the smaller monasteries to fund and endow colleges at Oxford and at his home town of Ipswich. In 1535, the Crown ordered an evaluation of the worth of the English houses, the *Valor Ecclesiasticus*; the stage was set for the anti-monastic campaign. 'Hence, when in 1535 the great visitation of the monasteries was undertaken under the supervision of Thomas Cromwell, the King's Vicar-General for ecclesiastical affairs,' Powicke remarked, 'the Crown had already in its possession a survey of monastic wealth and was using for the material control of the whole Church all the machinery of government, all the experience acquired by the exchequer and chancery during the previous centures.' In January 1536, Parliament set the quantitative definition of laxity and sin for English monasteries at £200 per annum, and dissolved those houses which failed to meet this standard. A Court of Augmentation was quickly created to facilitate the transfer of the monastic property to the Crown. The so-called 'greater monasteries' caught the attention of Henry's officials in 1537, and visitants were dispatched to convince these houses to dissolve themselves. Most offered no resistance to the King's wishes. 'Persuasion was seldom difficult, partly because everywhere it was rumoured that soon they would be suppressed, partly because some houses already found difficulty in continuing.' Finally, a parliamentary act

of 1539 declared that all monastic property surrendered after 1536 legally belonged to the Crown. The Henrician monks did not embrace the martyr's mantle, and they passively accepted their fate along with their pensions. A few individuals, however, questioned the royal policy; the Abbots of Colchester, Reading, and Glastonbury all protested, and were executed in 1539. Among other things, the short-lived Pilgrimage of Grace (1536-37) also reacted against the suppression of the smaller northern monasteries.

After Henry VIII's death in 1547, the course of the Reformation and the status of English Roman Catholics became confused. During Edward VI's reign (1547-1553), a more radical Protestant theology replaced Henry's conservatism: clergy were permitted to marry; images and statues destroyed; and chantries abolished. More radical than its 1549 counterpart, the *Prayer Book* of 1552 and the accompanying *Act of Uniformity* brought the English Reformation closer to continental practices. Then came an abrupt change: Mary Tudor succeeded her brother to the throne in 1553; the main objective of the reign being the restoration of Roman Catholicism. Mary presided over the repeal of the laws passed during the previous two reigns against the old religion, and in 1554 Reginald Pole absolved members of Parliament from their sins of schism. Moreover, the Queen re-established a monastery at Westminster, but the experiment did not survive the reign of her sister Elizabeth, who dissolved the community within two decades after her accession. Although the monastic lands were not returned to the Roman Church, Mary's brief reign did not endear Catholicism to her countrymen. Her marriage to Philip, King of Spain, the loss of Calais, and the needless burnings of Smithfield, turned Catholicism into a feared and hated religion. John Foxe made it certain that people would never forget the fiendish and cruel deeds of this Roman Catholic monarch. Unmourned and childless, Mary died on 17 November 1558, and was succeeded by her half-sister Elizabeth, the daughter of Ann Boleyn.

Elizabeth (1558-1603) tried to steer English religious life back to the days of her father and consequently tolerated some aspects of Roman Catholicism, but like Henry she rejected papal authority. During the first year of her reign, the *Act of Supremacy* declared Elizabeth the Supreme Governor of the Church of England, and later the *Act of Uniformity* required that all church and state officials must swear an oath of allegiance. This Act also stipulated that her clergy must conduct services according to *The Book of Common Prayer*, and a graduated penalty of imprisonment was imposed on those who refused. After the third conviction, for example, the guilty cleric faced the possibility of life imprisonment. Moreover, it became an offence to hear a Roman Catholic mass, and attendance at Anglican services was made mandatory.

Elizabeth wanted a compromise, and would tolerate no extremes. Both the Puritans returning home from exile on the continent and those who clung to the old order were subjected to restrictive legislation. But a series of domestic and external events – for example, the Northern Rebellion of 1569, the papal excommunication of Elizabeth in 1570, the Ridolfi plot, the intrigues of Mary Queen of Scots, and finally the Armada – especially marked the Roman Catholic as a potential traitor. And Parliament responded to this Catholic threat with a series of statutes. To declare the Queen a heretic or schismatic, or to convert or be converted to Roman Catholicism, carried the charge of treason. The penalties for attending mass or missing its Anglican counterpart were also increased. Harbouring recusants (that is, those who refused to attend Anglican services), became a crime, and convicted recusants were required to possess a licence to journey more than five miles from their home. The increasing flow of continentally trained priests and Jesuits into Anglican England produced the so-called 'act that made martyrs': it was a treasonable act for a native Englishman to return to his country unless he registered or declared himself within forty-eight hours of his arrival. Moreover, any person who assisted or helped a priest could be subjected to the same punishment; 'priest holes,' consequently, became an accepted part of the architecture of many Roman Catholic homes.

These laws, however, were never applied consistently or even rigorously. In some parts of the country, leniency muted the full force of law, and it appears that these penal laws were enforced most stringently when Parliament was in session. The demands of the Puritans for a presbyterian system may have posed a more serious threat to the security of the realm, but the animosity against Catholicism remained the stronger current in English life. During the reigns of Henry VIII and Elizabeth I approximately one hundred and sixty-four priests, including such luminaries as Edmund Campion and Richard Gwyn, were executed. Under the reign of Mary Tudor over two hundred and seventy-three of their countrymen were also executed. By the end of the sixteenth century, therefore, the civil and religious rights of English Roman Catholics had been curtailed. They had become second-class citizens, potential traitors, and superstitious people who owed a higher allegiance to a foreign, and at times hostile, Pope in Rome.

This reforming fever soon spread over the border into Scotland, where the corrupt fabric of the Roman Catholic Church had also been recognized. The burning of the 'heretic' George Wishart on the authority of David, Cardinal Beaton, and the subsequent murder of the Cardinal, demonstrated the intensity of the hatred boiling beneath the surface of Scottish life. The presence of the French and the real possibility of Scotland becoming a Roman Catholic satellite prompted Queen Elizabeth to quick and drastic action. She supported the 'Congregation of the Lord' with men and money, and eventually these Scottish leaders expelled the French and deposed the French Regent, Mary of Guise, in 1560. This political revolution heralded the beginning of the reformation of the Roman Catholic Church in Scotland. The Scottish Parliament outlawed the mass and prescribed the death penalty for the third offence. The Parliament renounced the authority of the Pope, and John Knox's *Confession of Faith* and *Book of Discipline* – Calvinistic in doctrine and liturgy – were adopted. Scottish monasteries were pillaged, and religious life became impossible through harsh legislation against the mass. The northern reformers set up the Scottish General Assembly and authorized *The Book of Common Order*, which was based on the Geneva model. The *Concordat of Leith* (1572) declared that all individuals who held ecclesiastical benefices had to subscribe to the articles of religion contained in *The Westminster Confession of Faith* and had to swear an oath affirming the Monarch's supreme authority. No Roman Catholic protest broke out in Scotland such as the Pilgrimage of Grace or the Northern Rebellion; even the return of Queen Mary in 1561 failed to galvanize support for the old religion. Her son James Stuart's religious preferences confused many.

English Catholics expected much when the Scottish King, James VI, succeeded Elizabeth in 1603 as James I of England. Some of James I's public statements, his flirtations with Spain, and the Catholicism of his wife,

Anne of Denmark, seemed to augur well for the future of English Catholicism. But the imprudent, zealous, and rash actions of some again linked their faith with treason and disloyalty. Roman Catholics were clearly implicated in the Bye Plot (1603), and Catholic priests and laymen emerged as ring-leaders in the Gunpowder Plot (1605). Several Jesuits, including their Superior in England, Henry Garnet, suffered the fate of traitors. Consequently, the government began to prepare new legislation to tighten up the Elizabethan penal laws: Roman Catholics were excluded from certain professions such as law and medicine, and barred from holding commissions in the army and navy; their movements within the country were severely curtailed; a sacramental test was now demanded, and an oath of allegiance which declared that 'the pope, neither of himself, nor by any authority of the church or see of Rome . . . hath any power or authority to depose the king' was required. Although the force of these laws was applied with unequal severity throughout the country, and some Roman Catholics even dared to practise their faith openly, the stigma of disloyalty still survived. The news that Prince Charles and the Earl of Buckingham had failed to cement a marriage agreement with Roman Catholic Spain sparked bonfires and rejoicing in London, and demonstrated the intensity of the suspicion of many Englishmen towards Roman Catholicism. In Scotland, the earlier penal laws against Catholics were also strengthened and new measures passed; for example, laws against hiding priests and a prohibition against Scottish children being sent to Catholic colleges or to the continent were enacted.

An aerial view of Westminster Cathedral

English Catholics again anticipated the beginning of a new era of freedom and a relaxation of prohibitive legislation with the accession of Charles I, and with few exceptions the machinery of the penal laws did slow down. The public displays of Roman Catholicism by Queen Henrietta Maria, whose retinue included a bishop and several French priests, encouraged Catholics to practise their faith openly, if discreetly. The stormy relations between the Crown and Parliament dwarfed the urgency to enforce the legal restrictions against Catholics. When the Civil War finally erupted, some leading Roman Catholics supported the claims of the Stuart dynasty, although both sides in the conflict continued to collect fines against Catholics as a way to increase the size of their war chests! The victorious Puritans relaxed laws dealing with mandatory church attendance, but restrictions against Roman Catholics, who still aroused their suspicion, were not lightened. During the Interregnum, moreover, many English associated the papists with the royal cause.

When the third Stuart, Charles II, landed at Dover in 1660, many Catholics again believed that the new monarch would look favourably on their religion. Some of his statements from the continent, the *Declaration of Breda*, the secret Treaty of Dover with France and his marriage to Catherine of Braganza, all raised Catholic expectations and hopes, but the legislation from his Protestant parliament represented a victory for the Anglicans against Roman Catholicism and the various Puritan sects which flourished during the previous decades. The Clarendon Code, a series of statutes aimed at the non-Conformists, also curtailed the civil and religious liberties of England's Catholic community: the *Corporation Act* (1661) required municipal office holders to take the Anglican sacrament yearly; the *Act of Uniformity* (1662) demanded that clergymen use the Prayer Book, which was modified in 1660 for religious services; the *Five Mile Act* (1665) excluded dissenters from teaching and prohibited them from coming within five miles of a town; and the *Conventicle Act* (1664) limited attendance at non-Anglican services to four. Charles' open espousal of Roman Catholicism, his intention to suspend several laws against the papists and the haunting fear that James, the King's Catholic brother, might spawn a Roman dynasty, drove the loyal Anglicans in the House of Commons to seek new repressive measures. The *Test Act* (1673), consequently, required all who held civil or military office to receive the Anglican sacrament, to swear oaths of loyalty and allegiance to the Crown, and to make a declaration against transubstantiation which stated, ' . . . I do not believe that there is any transubstantiation in the Sacrament of the Lord's Supper, or in the elements of bread and wine, at or after the consecration thereof by any person whatsoever.' Finally the *Test Act* (1678) excluded all Roman Catholics from Parliament.

Moreover, Roman Catholicism did not fare well outside the walls of the Anglican-controlled House of Commons. Some blamed the London fire of 1666 on the city's Catholics, but 'the Popish Plot' had more serious implications. Titus Oates, a rogue and consummate liar and a former Anabaptist, had converted to Catholicism but after a chequered career he turned to the Church of England. In 1678, he started a national panic by announcing that he had uncovered the plot which aimed to assassinate Charles II and place his Roman Catholic brother on the throne. The Society of Jesus, of course, emerged as the chief conspirators. The panic lasted until 1681, and unleashed a tide of hatred and cries for vengeance against Roman Catholics.

Many were imprisoned, and numerous Catholics executed for their alleged involvement in the plot. Oliver Plunket, the Archbishop of Armagh, was one of them, and became the last priest executed at Tyburn for his religion.

Much to the embarrassment and disgust of his co-religious, who wanted to practise their faith quietly and unobtrusively, the Roman Catholic James II, who converted in 1670 and succeeded his brother in 1685, flaunted his religion. (Parliament had sought to exclude him from the throne, but without success.) James appointed Roman Catholics to positions in the government, the army and universities. To the sensitive and suspicious Anglican, this appeared as another plot to re-introduce Catholicism by royal fiat, which must be resisted. In 1687, the King rashly issued a *Declaration of Indulgence* which proclaimed religious liberty throughout the kingdom and suspended the operation of the penal laws against Catholics. The birth of a male heir transformed the possibility of a Roman Catholic dynasty into a reality, and so began the process known as the Glorious Revolution. William of Orange accepted the crown in defence of the country's religious and constitutional liberties, and became joint monarch with his wife Mary; James fled into exile. Fearing reprisals from this thoroughly Protestant prince, many English Catholics also fled to the Continent, but William and Mary (daughter of James II) used statute law and not the gallows to defend the Anglican establishment of their country. Acts of Parliament strengthened the exclusion of Catholics from certain areas of the legal profession and required Roman Catholics to register their property, which was more heavily taxed than non-Catholic land.

The laying of the foundation stone

Concessions were made, however, to the Protestant Dissenters. In an attempt to unite all non-Conformists in opposition to James II the *Toleration Act* of 1689 granted them some religious freedom. With their emergence Roman Catholics also began to be accepted as responsible citizens. Accusations that some Catholics had actively supported the 1715 rising failed to ignite the fires of hatred as such a charge would earlier have done. And some Catholic priests did offer mass for the success of the 1745 Rebellion, but the Stuart magic had worn thin with English Catholics and large numbers failed to flock to the Stuart standard; so died the cause of Prince Charles.

With the Hanoverians came real signs of relaxation, and gradually Roman Catholics began to gain religious and civil parity with other denominations. In 1778, Catholics could own property provided that they took an oath – but one which did not involve a denial or rejection of their religious beliefs, and the harsh penalties for operating Catholic schools were relaxed. This legislation, however, occasioned the last great outburst of anti-Catholic hatred. Armed with a petition demanding the repeal of the 1778 *Relief Act*, and leading a large and angry 'no popery' mob, Lord George Gordon approached the Parliament buildings at Westminster during the summer of 1780. Some rioting and looting broke out, and the military had to dislodge the protesters who had by then taken control of the City of London.

In spite of this and other isolated outbursts, the government continued to repeal the restrictive laws; English Roman Catholics had proved their loyalty over the centuries, and their patriotism should be rewarded. By 1791, they were considered safe. Consequently, 'Catholics who took the oath of allegiance were free from disabilities relating to education, property, and the practice of law. Catholic peers were given the right of access to the the king; they were permitted attendance at religious services and were allowed to enter religious orders.'[7] These rights were also extended to Irish and Scottish Catholics. In 1817, commissions to all ranks of the army and navy were opened to Catholics. Catholicism, therefore, had survived the attacks of the Reformation and the restrictions of the penal laws and, indeed, 'maintained its continuity through an age of unprecedented upheaval.'[8] John Bossy interpreted the struggles of the post-Reformation Catholic Church in England not as a 'process of continuous decline reaching its nadir in the eighteenth century, but as a patient and continuous process of construction from small beginnings in which the eighteenth century represents a phase of modest progress and of careful preparation for the future.'[9] Moreover, the early years of the nineteenth century represented a 'take-off' period for English Catholics. One of the crucial and emotional debates of these years concerned the rights of Catholics to sit in Parliament.

The story of Catholic emancipation was intimately connected with England's stormy and troublesome relationship with Ireland. Pitt's desire to unite the Parliaments of England and Ireland resulted in the *Act of Union* of 1801. To secure the support of the Irish members for the abolition of their assembly, the Prime Minister hinted at the possibility of Catholic emancipation. But Pitt's bill, drafted in 1801, floundered because of George III's belief that his assent would violate the provisions of his coronation oath. The campaign for Catholic emancipation, however, did not die. It did attract some support in England, but the lingering fear and suspicion of Roman Catholicism meant that any act must contain some securities to protect the Anglican state. The most important of which concerned the right of the English government to exercise a veto on ecclesiastical appointments by Rome. Meanwhile, personalities and events in Ireland continued to act as catalysts. The English hierarchy agreed to the compromise of a veto, but Daniel O'Connell and the Irish bishops successfully argued that this concession would destroy the independence of the Catholic Church. The charismatic O'Connell used the Catholic Association and the funds from Catholic rents to campaign throughout Ireland for emancipation. His electoral victory over Vesey Fitzgerald in County Clare during July 1828 forced Wellington, the Prime Minister, and Robert Peel to retract their earlier opposition to Catholic emancipation.

The earlier repeal of the Test and Corporation Acts in 1828 provided a precedent for this concession to Catholics, but the prospect of a civil war in Ireland if O'Connell did not take his seat finally pushed the Tories to concede. Wellington's threat of resignation forced George IV to withdraw his opposition to the bill. Despite protests from organizations such as the Brunswick Clubs that the English constitution was in danger, the *Catholic Emancipation Act* received the royal assent in 1829. Roman Catholics were again admitted to most public offices, save those of the Lord Chancellor, Keeper of the Great Seal, Lord Lieutenant of Ireland, and the High Commissioner of the Church of Scotland. Other securities were included to safeguard the established church. Catholic bishops, for example, were forbidden to take a title of a see already claimed by the Anglican hierarchy. The Act also outlawed public religious services conducted by Roman Catholics. A clause which sought to strangle the growth of the Jesuits and other religious orders was more rhetoric than forcible in law. Finally, Roman Catholics elected to Parliament had to swear an oath that they would not subvert the established church. Fearing that Irish Catholics might swamp the House of Commons, and also hoping to preserve the Protestant ascendency in Ireland, the Act radically altered the Irish franchise: the voting qualification was raised from the traditional forty shillings to a prohibitive £10.

With very few exceptions, English Roman Catholics had finally re-claimed their birthright, after centuries of being penalized for their faith. Many believed that Rome should also recognize their vitality, stability and accomplishments, and re-establish the hierarchy in England. The question of ecclesiastical authority in England had always presented a problem for Rome. When it became apparent that the reformers could not succeed in expunging Roman Catholicism from English soil, the Pope appointed a cleric in 1598 with the title of Archpriest to govern the secular priests in the country. But the traditional jealousy between the secular and religious priests soon erupted. According to the secular clergy, George Blackwell the first Archpriest, favouring the Jesuits, ignored them, and jeopardized the interests of English Catholicism because of his pro-Jesuit policies. Consequently, a group of secular priests, the Appellants, wrote to Rome in 1599 and asked for Blackwell's removal.

The controversy lasted for years and saw several Archpriests trying to govern and administer English Catholicism. In 1623, Rome experimented with the appointment of William Bishop as Vicar Apostolic. Some problems arose, and the feud between the seculars and religious continued to divide Catholicism. In 1685, John Lyburn was appointed Vicar Apostolic, and after three years the country was divided into four geographic districts: London, Midland, Northern, and Western. Rome increased the number of Vicars Apostolic to eight in 1840, many Catholics beginning to regard this institution as a temporary arrangement until Rome could reconstitute an English hierarchy. Scottish interests were initially supervised by the Archpriest in England. Some Scots, however, worked to free the Catholic Church in Scotland from authority south of the border, and several proposals were discussed. Finally, on 16 March 1694, Pope Innocent XII appointed Thomas Nicolson as the first Vicar Apostolic in Scotland. Like its English counterpart, the Scottish institution increased in numbers until there were three districts in 1827.

By the middle of the nineteenth century, English Roman Catholics demanded their freedom and independence from the Propaganda in Rome. England should no longer be regarded in Roman eyes as missionary territory; it must, therefore, have a proper hierarchy. The Vicars Apostolic and the clergy desired the re-establishment of a hierarchy, but for different and conflicting reasons. 'While the vicars apostolic wanted a hierarchy because they wanted freedom from Rome, their clergy wanted a hierarchy to secure more freedom from vicars-apostolic.'[10] Under the missionary set-up, for example, priests could be moved from place to place at the whim of the Vicar Apostolic. Rome, however, refused to act on these requests, part of the reason for which can be found in the arguments of Cardinal Action, who told Roman authorities that a hierarchy would destroy the fragile structure of English Catholicism. After his death in 1847 the last obstacle was removed.

The long awaited creation of an English hierarchy was scheduled for late 1847, but the plan was suddenly postponed. Rome's sensitivity to conditions in England

An early view of the front facade, doors draped

and the history of Catholicism in the country asserted themselves. Certain prerequisites must be met before the establishment of the hierarchy: a Whig government must be in power; Parliament must be in recess; and the new Catholic dioceses must avoid those ancient titles associated with the established church. The year 1850 was optimum, but 'the actual timing proved nothing less than tragic.'[11] Because of John Henry Newman's recent conversion (in 1845) and the scandal caused by the Gorham case of 1850, many Anglicans believed that the restoration of a Catholic hierarchy constituted nothing less than a frontal attack on the established church. In September 1850, however, Pope Pius IX issued the brief which established thirteen sees in England, and shortly afterwards he created Nicholas Wiseman Cardinal Archbishop of Westminster.

This papal action, the new Cardinal's pastoral *Out of the Flaminian Gate*, and his inopportune rhetoric, occasioned a harsh rebuke in *The Times*, some no-popery riots, and Lord John Russell's fiery 'Durham Letter'. But the energy and intensity of this reaction could not be sustained. The government's ill-timed and unfortunate *Ecclesiastical Titles Act* (1851) attacked 'Papal Aggression' by making the creation of territorial titles illegal. This law, however, was a dead letter and a sham, and was repealed by Gladstone in 1871. In 1878, Pope Leo XIII re-established the Roman Catholic hierarchy in Scotland.

Newman's comment about English Roman Catholicism's 'second spring' captured the euphoria and self-confidence of Catholics in England. Despite some real tensions within Catholicism for example, the increasing strength of the clergy in church affairs at the expense of the laity, the triumph of Ultramontanism over the traditional Catholic spirit, and the challenge to old and accepted ways by the increasing number of converts to Catholicism, it had successfully survived centuries of persecution and legal disabilities, and had even regained some of its lost status. Notable converts, such as Newman, Manning, and Lord Ripon, added to the respectability and vitality of the faith. The number of churches, schools and convents increased. Religious orders flourished. Catholic clergy shed their timidity and began to take an active part in educational and social reforms. English Roman Catholicism had a right to be proud of its achievements: only a temple or a shrine could adequately capture this buoyancy and sense of accomplishment.

2. A CATHEDRAL FOR WESTMINSTER

A cathedral in central London, many English Catholics agreed, was needed not only to provide a place of worship for the faithful of the metropolis, but also to provide a visible monument to the respectability and achievements of their religion. 'The outward symbol of this ability to build well and expensively was Westminster Cathedral.'[1] Moreover, some Roman Catholics wanted a permanent monument to their first archbishop of the industrial age, Nicholas Wiseman. His successor, Cardinal Henry Manning, saw other priorities, and his dedication to the eradication of poverty in London meant that a new cathedral might have to be sacrificed. Manning believed that 'the work of saving these children was his first duty, the first duty of the Catholics of London.'[2] As he remarked elsewhere, 'Could I leave 20,000 children without education and drain my friends to pile up stones and bricks?'[3] Cathedral–building represented an expensive relic associated with medieval civilizations: 'I have been content with my Old Sarum and my Selsey. The days of Salisbury and Chichester are to come.'[4] Purcell captured Archbishop Manning's thoughts on a new cathedral:

> A memorial church to Cardinal Wiseman belonged to the past, but the saving of Catholic children from the Protestant workhouses or reformatories, where their faith would be lost, belonged to the present and the future, and he made this saving work the primary end and aim of his labours.[5]

Although Cardinal Manning discouraged building an 'arch of triumph before the battle was won',[6] and

View from the south east

openly acknowledged the urgent need to educate the children of his archdiocese, he nonetheless recognized that a cathedral had to be constructed in the future.

In 1867, Manning purchased some property in Carlisle Place for £16,500, and began to discuss plans for a cathedral to be built on a modest scale.[7] When he acquired another nearby piece of property, his vision also began to expand: the future cathedral must now be patterned along the lines of Cologne Cathedral. But Cardinal Manning lacked the funds to flesh-out his dream. In 1882 a promise from a wealthy layman to finance the cathedral failed to materialize, but even though the funds eluded him, Manning did not abandon hope. A year later, the Cardinal again demonstrated his support for a Roman Catholic cathedral in central London. 'Opposite the windows of his residence and adjoining the land he had already purchased, stood the Middlesex County Prison of Tothill fields';[8] Cardinal Manning found out that the site was for sale. He believed that the four-acre property would prove to be a better investment for the future cathedral than the land he had previously bought. Consequently, he sold the old site, collected another £20,000, and took out a mortgage to acquire the grounds of the former prison for approximately £115,000. But Cardinal Manning could never scrape together enough money to begin the actual construction; accordingly his successor at Westminster, Herbert Vaughan, accepted the challenge.

'Like Manning's, Vaughan's reputation has rather suffered at the hands of subsequent assessors of his work.'[9] As a result of this, the personality of Herbert Vaughan emerges as a humourless administrator, an individual more at home with fund-raising drives, immersed in the world of debits and credits rather than in a ministry of personal contacts and relationships.

The stereotype of Cardinal Vaughan sounds brutal: '. . . a man who was coldly efficient, a nuts-and-bolts administrator, too distant to be likeable.'[10] These opinions, however, do contain some elements of truth. Vaughan was a scrupulous and skilful administrator and organizer. Suffocated by the administrative responsibilities at Salford, and then at Westminster, and also because of ill-health, Vaughan never enjoyed popularity with his priests who thought that their spiritual leader was cool and aloof. But this caricature is too harsh. The needs of people, as well as the cost of bricks and mortar, also consumed Cardinal Vaughan's time and energy.

Herbert Alfred Vaughan was born into an old established Roman Catholic family on 15 April 1832, in Gloucester. His mother, a convert, prayed that all her children would become priests or enter the convent. And it appears that her prayers were answered: six of her eight sons became priests, and four of her daughters became nuns. Herbert, the eldest son, experienced England's religious orders early in life. For the five years between 1841 and 1846 young Vaughan was educated at Stonyhurst; subsequently at another Jesuit school in Belgium. But he also had close contacts with the Benedictines. He spent a year as a student with the monks at Downside Abbey and his brother Joseph eventually joined the Benedictines of that house. In 1851, Herbert Vaughan went to Rome to continue his studies for the priesthood, being ordained in October 1854. It was in Italy that his close friendship began with the recent convert from Anglicanism, Henry Manning, which would later influence his career in the church.

On his return to England, Vaughan went to St. Edmund's, Ware, where he served as vice-president, later joining Manning's Oblates. Four years later, he resigned this post because of ecclesiastical in-fighting which resulted in the departure of the Oblates from St. Edmund's. A desire to minister to the world's heathen population soon grew into an obsession with the young and idealistic cleric, and for nearly two years (1863-1865) Vaughan travelled throughout North and South America trying to raise enough money to establish a college in England to train foreign missionaries. The trip proved successful, and patrons promised more money after his return to England in July 1865. A year later, St. Joseph's College, Mill Hill, opened its doors. In November 1871, Vaughan triumphantly accompanied several Mill Hill Missionaries to America, where they began work among that country's black population.

But Vaughan was not destined to direct grand missionary projects. Manning, who became Archbishop of Westminster in 1865, chose Herbert Vaughan as the new Bishop of Salford. Unknown in the North, Vaughan owed this appointment to his long friendship with the Cardinal because 'by this time all appointments to the English hierarchy had effectively become Manning's appointments.'[11] Vaughan's accomplishments at Salford were noteworthy: a pastoral seminary to prepare priests for work in the cities; annual diocesan synods which, among other duties, co-ordinated various fund-raising programs; and the creation of numerous new parishes, to name but a few.[12] Bishop Vaughan went to Rome and argued for the rights of bishops against the Jesuits, who claimed certain exemptions from episcopal supervision and opened a grammar school in Manchester without Vaughan's permission. His influence helped to produce *Romanos Pontifices* (1881) which upheld the rights of his fellow bishops against the Jesuits. Alarmed by the so-called 'leakage' which drained children from the Roman

View from the west

faith, Bishop Vaughan founded the Catholic Protection and Rescue Society in 1886 'to save the children by providing alternative social relief from that given by the workhouses and the Protestant philanthropic bodies.'[13] Vaughan established soup kitchens, night shelters, and encouraged numerous other schemes for the poor in his diocese. He also attacked the problem of drink by advocating a reduction in the licenses given to public houses.

If Vaughan's appointment to Salford caused some consternation in Roman Catholic circles, the announcement in 1892 that he would succeed his friend at Westminster was generally expected, and it met with the approval of the English bishops. A year later he was created a Cardinal. In addition to his administrative skills, his accomplishments as Archbishop of Westminster matched his impressive achievements in the North. Catholic education still remained one of his favourite projects. Archbishop Vaughan closed down the diocesan seminary at Hammersmith, but he actively supported the establishment of a central one at New Oscott in the Midlands to serve several dioceses; it opened in 1893. Vaughan had approved the ban on Roman Catholics going to Oxford and Cambridge, but he eventually changed his mind and persuaded the other English bishops to approach Rome and petition to have the prohibition lifted, which was done in 1895. He also campaigned for the 1902 *Education Act*, which acknowledged the rights of denominational schools to government support. In the area of theology and ecclesiastical policy, Cardinal Vaughan became the outspoken critic of the reunion movement, and against the efforts of Anglo-Catholics and some Roman Catholics to have Anglican orders declared valid. It was through his efforts in England and Rome that Anglican orders were declared 'null and void' in 1896. In the opinion of some, however, the construction of Westminster Cathedral ranked as his greatest single achievement.

When Vaughan[14] became Archbishop of Westminster in 1892, he brought to his large urban archdiocese a sense of triumphalism, loyalty to Rome, and a commitment to educational and financial reforms. But dedication to the construction of a new cathedral also coloured his tenure in office: '... he immediately decided as his major project, to build a cathedral which would be a liturgical, pastoral and intellectual center for English Catholicism.'[15] The overdue recognition for the progress of Roman Catholics in Britain was the motivation, and 'the building of Westminster Cathedral was both symbolic of his general attitude as well as an example of his administrative ability.'[16] According to his biographer, Vaughan wanted a 'Cathedral which should be the head and heart of the life of the Church in England, and the vivifying centre of its spirit and worship.' Moreover, 'it was to be the home of a companionship of priests, the example of whose lives should colour all the ideals and activities of the diocese.'[17] This new church must necessarily become the spiritual centre of England. Lecturers would address the faithful, meeting-space would be available for clubs, and dedicated clergy would minister to the special needs of the London area. Because of his untiring efforts and the financial contributions of numerous eager Roman Catholics, Westminster Cathedral emerged from dream to reality.

The construction of this cathedral became one of Vaughan's top priorities. According to one of his biographers, 'Cardinal Vaughan told his cousin at St. Pancras when he arrived in London from Salford as Archbishop-elect, his biggest project was to build a cathedral in Westminster.'[18] The property for the cathedral had been secured, some money already collected or pledged, and numerous influential Roman Catholics had openly endorsed the scheme, but Vaughan realized that his building project might invite some criticism. Cardinal Manning had already wrestled with the strong emotional critique which haunted Vaughan: money lavished on a church robbed the poor, and should be given instead to a charitable organization. But other voices of opposition also confronted Cardinal Vaughan. Some argued that the age of cathedrals belonged to the Middle Ages, while others maintained that the project failed to capture the imagination of the rank and file of Roman Catholics needed to finance the construction of this grand church. Some sceptics observed that the undertaking might prove an embarrassment to English Catholics rather than a proud symbol of accomplishment. They doubted the Cardinal's ability to complete the project, and believed that an unfinished folly, not a proper cathedral, would greet Londoners in Victoria Street.

In spite of these misgivings, Cardinal Vaughan did not waver. He used the Catholic press to drum up support and began a fund-raising drive. In 1894, J F Bentley was named as the architect, and immediately set out for Italy to study firsthand the country's numerous churches and basilicas. The design had also been chosen: it was to be in the Byzantine tradition. Several reasons contributed to this decision. Unlike the more popular and ubiquitous Gothic, a Byzantine church did not have to be completed in sections; the shell could be finished first, and then attention could be focused on interior decorations.[19] More importantly, the Byzantine style was cheaper to construct than its Gothic or Baroque counterparts. Success shined on Cardinal Vaughan's efforts, and the first important stage of construction began in the summer of 1895.

With pomp and grandeur, Cardinal Herbert Vaughan solemnly blessed the foundation stone of his new cathedral. This action signalled the beginning of the long – awaited construction of the new Roman Catholic cathedral in central London. At a celebration following the impressive ceremony, Vaughan sketched his plans for the future of his metropolitan church. This was to be no ordinary place of worship. Vaughan pointed out 'that the Catholic body must have a Cathedral in which the sacred liturgy of the church should be carried out in all its fulness day by day, and many times a day, as it was of old in Westminster and in Canterbury.'[20] The ecclesiastical and lay dignitaries present greeted this vision with applause.

If Vaughan wanted to bring back the glories of the pre-Reformation Catholic Church to Britain, then he could not ignore the English Benedictine Congregation. As in the days before the destruction of the Henrician reforms, monks must breathe life into this new Westminster. And English monks were eager to accommodate the Archbishop's wish. Vaughan revealed that his 'anxiety with regard to the Cathedral was allayed by the readiness with which he found the English Benedictine Fathers, full of life and energy and numbers, ready to come back to Westminster.'[21] The monks of St. Gregory's, Downside, whom the Cardinal knew and admired, would supply the manpower. The suburb of Ealing in West London, would be a suitable location for these Benedictines, who would take charge of the liturgy in Vaughan's cathedral.

Cardinal Vaughan's plan was simple: '. . . while safeguarding the position and rights of the Chapter, to hand over the whole working and management of the Cathedral to the monks.'[22] As in the Middle Ages the cathedral would be staffed by the Black Monks. A Prior would be the immediate superior, and Vaughan would enjoy the privileges and jurisdiction of an Abbot. According to his biographer, this vision '. . . at one time certainly represented what the Cardinal meant when he spoke of the Benedictines coming back to Westminster.' Moreover, Vaughan wanted to hand over 'to the Benedictines the two missions in Westminster, which would ultimately be incorporated in the Cathedral parish, so that they might become familiar with the district they would have to work in when the Cathedral was opened.'[23] Cardinal Vaughan maintained that 'there could be no higher or holier work any body of men could be called upon to undertake, and he still unhesitatingly counted on the co-operation of the monks.'[24]

To bring the Benedictine monks to London was the first step. Their community had settled at Downside near Bath in 1814, and by the 1890's the community had grown to a mature membership. The monks were committed to missionary work and the conversion of England to Roman Catholicism.[25] In May 1896 Cardinal Vaughan informed the superior of Downside Abbey, Prior Edmund Ford, that he was 'disposed to give' a mission in Ealing to the Benedictines of that monastery.[26] He also told Ford that a proper site for this new foundation could easily be purchased there.[27] Ford's answer was short: 'as soon as I can I will go and see Ealing.' The Downside superior also indicated that he entertained his own vision for the future of the Benedictines in London: 'Your Eminence would I presume wish us to try and do more than merely take charge of the mission?'[28] If Benedictines from Downside settled in London, they must be involved in active parish work in addition to their ceremonial duties at the cathedral.

View from the north west

Rendering the liturgy of Westminster Cathedral exclusively was inappropriate.[29]

Hugh Ford was born on 23 March 1851 at Clifton Park. When he was ten, his parents sent him to Downside School, which at that time had an enrolment of over fifty students. Staffed by the monks, Downside could proudly boast of several famous men who were educated at the Benedictine school, such as the future Bishop of Birmingham, William Ullathorne, and Roger Vaughan, the future Bishop of Sydney. Herbert Vaughan, who wanted the Downside monks to come to Westminster, had also attended the school. His biographer quotes a contemporary who described young Ford as 'a pale delicate-looking boy, prim and precise in manner and dress, not like other boys, more thoughtful and quick.'[30] Believing that he had a Benedictine vocation, he entered the novitiate at Belmont in November 1868, and took Edmund for his religious name. Three years later, Edmund Ford made his solemn profession as a monk. Illness, however, forced him to interrupt his studies at Belmont, and he returned to Downside in 1871.

Because of his questionable health, Minor Orders were postponed, but he made his solemn profession on 24 January 1873. During the same year, his superiors decided that a sea voyage and long holiday might provide a cure for the sickly young monk, and in November he left for Australia. After he returned to Downside in 1876, Dom Edmund was appointed Sub-Prefect, a position which carried with it the responsibility for discipline throughout the school. Ford's health seemed to improve, and he was ordained deacon in 1877, and priest the following year. It appeared that his career would be in education. Appointed Prefect of Studies in 1878, he began to introduce lay masters into the school and also instituted a board with lay membership which discussed school policy. In 1884, Dom Edmund was sent to Rome with two confreres to start a house of studies for his congregation; his stay in Italy lasted only one year.

Ordered back by the President of the English Benedictine Congregation, Dom Edmund served a brief term as Prior of Downside (1885-1888). According to his biographer, these were years of growth and development for Downside. Improvement in the physical plant, expansion of the school, and the opening of the Lady Chapel were supervised by Prior Ford. In 1889, the ex-prior took up residence at the Benedictine mission at Beccles. But he was soon back at Downside; in July 1894 he was again chosen as Prior. During the foundation stone ceremony at Westminster Cathedral, Prior Ford heard and approved of Cardinal Vaughan's dreams about monks conducting the services at his new cathedral. Both churchmen, therefore, relished the thought of a Benedictine presence at Westminster Cathedral, but Ford had strong views about the nature of the work and the extent of the involvement of his monks in London.

The Prior maintained that a Benedictine presence in the capital was imperative, but any rash or unplanned action would be harmful. A man of prudence, Ford was not mesmerized by the imagination and idealism of Cardinal Vaughan. 'I cannot but express to your Eminence our grateful acknowledgement for offering us the work that you suggest at Ealing,' he wrote to the Cardinal, 'and our appreciation of the confidence placed in us by entrusting it to us . . .'[31] Work for the monks, however, must be found: 'Your Eminence will recognize the dangers in establishing a religious community without sufficient occupation for its members and the consequent difficulty in maintaining a religious spirit. . . Hence I feel,' he continued, 'a scruple in sending a religious anywhere without assigning a definite work that he could and would do.'

In the future, Ford suggested, a school might be a possibility, but parish work must definitely supplement the choral duties of Westminster Cathedral. Consequently, 'we may have a flourishing community at Ealing' in a few years. Ford concluded his letter to Vaughan by pointing out that pastoral work in Ealing would not detract from liturgical duties in London. 'I would add that the establishment of a house at Ealing would not render it more difficult to find men for the Cathedral, on the contrary it would I think render it easier by providing another community from which to draw when the time comes.'[32] Ford's position was, therefore, clear. He would gladly assign monks for Westminster Cathedral, but only if pastoral duties formed part of the agreement.

Within a fortnight, Cardinal Vaughan responded favourably to Prior Ford's conditions. Vaughan would welcome the monks in Ealing if certain conditions were met: 'Provided the consent of the Holy See be obtained,'[33] Ford was authorised to lay a foundation at Ealing provided that the new monastery 'is not to include the opening of any school other than a Public Elementary School'; the monks would provide for the spiritual needs of the area and live a conventual life; if the foundation did not succeed in five years, the Archbishop would repay the Benedictines the amount spent on housing and the property; and finally, the monks must agree to sing the Divine Office at Westminster Cathedral. The Cardinal was explicit and forceful on this point. 'One of the principal reasons inducing

A foreshortened view of the campanile

the Cardinal Archbishop to invite the Benedictines to open a house at Ealing,' he concluded in his letter to Ford, 'is that they may be sufficiently near to Westminster to contribute to the choral service of the Cathedral.'[34] If these guidelines were acceptable to the Downside Benedictines, Cardinal Vaughan would welcome the monks into his archdiocese. Edmund Ford, however, had won a major concession: his monks would sing their breviary in the stalls of Westminster; but they would also work at a nearby parish in Ealing. Ford's next step was to secure the permission of the Abbot President of the English Benedictine Congregation and his council.

With Vaughan's offer of 17 June 1896, Prior Edmund Ford wrote to Dom Anselm O'Gorman, the President, and his advisers, presenting strong arguments in favour of sending Benedictine monks to London.[35] Monks could live a community life at Ealing, conduct an urban parish, and be near to their liturgical obligations at Westminster Cathedral. 'It is said to be one of the best districts near London still unoccupied as a parish,' Ford argued, and 'the district is rapidly developing and will have the character of a high class suburb.'[36] Moreover, monks could take the fifteen minute trip on the Great Western Railway to central London and their work at the cathedral. Within a month, the President of the English Benedictine Congregation had informed Ford that the Council had 'decided unanimously to accept the foundation which was offered, as well as the monastery to be built successively, and eventually the mission of the place called Ealing . . .'[37] Ford, immediately petitioned Pope Leo XIII: 'Having obtained the permission from the Superiors of our Congregation, as well as the assent of . . . the Cardinal Archbishop of Westminster, we humbly implore from the Holy See the faculty to found in Ealing a new residence, as well as to build later a monastery, and eventually to accept from the same Cardinal the mission of the same place Ealing.'[38] On 28 October 1896, Cardinal Vaughan informed Edmund Ford that he had 'received the necessary permission from the Holy See for you to take Ealing: the conditions being those we agreed upon.'[39]

It appeared that Cardinal Vaughan's dream to have Benedictine monks associated with his new cathedral, as they had been with the old, would come to fruition. Downside had given its approval to the project, and began to appoint members of the community to the new Ealing mission. In 1896, Prior Ford purchased two acres of land and a stately dwelling, Castle Hill House, for the new Ealing Benedictine community. On 13 March 1897, Dom Bernard Bulbeck arrived, and began to minister to the Roman Catholics of the area. Both the Archbishop and the Prior treasured their plans for the new Benedictine monastery, but problems and conflicts soon developed.

Vaughan's biographer argues that the Archbishop almost immediately recognized difficulties in the arrangements he had made with the Downside Benedictines. Westminster Cathedral was to be no ordinary church, but 'a Cathedral in the heart of the Empire, making its appeal to a vast multitude and destined for the service of a whole people.'[40] Consequently, 'it seemed incongruous that such a national centre of spiritual and far-reaching activities as he hoped the Cathedral would become, should be under the control of any single Religious Order, however ancient and however distinguished.'[41] Most importantly, the secular clergy resented the invasion of these monks.

Cardinal Vaughan had tried to be especially sensitive to the feelings of his Cathedral Chapter. In 1894, for example, the Chapter had been informed that 'the Cardinal was arranging conditions to safeguard the rights of the Chapter in the new Cathedral, in view of the appointment of the Benedictines to carry on the services.'[42] The Chapter, however, was uneasy. At one of their regular monthly meetings, on 8 January 1895, attention was directed to the question of the Benedictines, and the secretary 'was requested to seek for and bring any notes of a meeting held at Archbishop's House when the plan was first proposed by His Eminence in 1894.'[43] The Chapter again discussed the question of the monks at the following month's meeting. It was at this time that the secretary admitted that he could not find those minutes which outlined the conditions proposed by the Cardinal to safeguard the rights of the Chapter. Vaughan continued to inform this body of the progress concerning the monks. In October 1896 the Chapter was given a copy of the Cardinal's offer to Prior Ford[44] to settle in Ealing,[45] and during the next meeting he informed the Chapter that he had received the rescript from Rome which sanctioned the foundation of the Benedictines in the archdiocese.[46] Cardinal Vaughan clearly remained committed to Benedictines conducting the Divine Office at Westminster Cathedral. That would be the extent of their responsibilities; the secular clergy would manage the other affairs of the cathedral.[47] Edmund Ford also had certain definite plans for his monks at Westminster Cathedral.

On 7 December 1898, Ford wrote to Cardinal Vaughan enclosing a series of proposals, asking him, 'to write to me any remarks thereon which may enable me to revise them in a form which would meet with your Eminence's approval and which with your consent I could lay before our fathers.'[48] Ford maintained that he framed these suggestions 'with the hope that they may prevent friction and quarrels in the future.' He offered Vaughan an escape from the association of the monks with the daily affairs of the cathedral: 'With this view, I would leave each Archbishop free from any obligation to employ the monks in any way unless he chose to do so, so that at the death of each Archbishop the right of the monks to carry on any work in or connected with the Cathedral would cease.' In Ford's mind, however, this would not diminish the importance or significance of the Benedictine presence. 'On the other hand I suggest that the monastery at Westminster should be founded by your Eminence, i.e., that you should secure us in our residence there with certain endowments and the use of one of the Chapels in the Cathedral . . . and that of this minimum no Archbishop should be able to deprive us.'

Ford argued for the right of the Benedictines to engage in pastoral work at the cathedral, but the duties entailed (for example, the number of daily masses, confessions, homilies and, of course, the portions of the Divine Office to be sung) should be carefully defined and agreed upon by both the monks and the ordinary. Moreover, 'the monks would have no claim to do the above works; each Archbishop would be free to exact these duties or not as he pleased. Anything beyond these specific duties would be matter of mutual agreement between the monks and each Archbishop.'[49] Ford believed that the new London foundation should have between a dozen and twenty members, and that each should be paid a yearly salary of £120, which 'is not excessive, considering the position and the necessary expenses of the position, beyond the personal expense of the men.'[50] The Archbishop should take the responsibility for all the revenues and the maintenance of the cathedral, but 'some portion of the revenue should be paid by him to the monks varying according to the work which they may be doing.'[51] Ford concluded his letter to the Archbishop, maintaining that two principles were important: 'the Archbishop ought to feel that the whole revenue of the church belongs to his administration and the monks ought to be given some direct pecuniary interest in the receipts of the Cathedral.'[52]

Cardinal Vaughan initially agreed to this proposal, but difficulties quickly appeared. According to Snead-Cox, 'the more the Cardinal considered the problems incidental to the activities of a double set of clergy, serving under separate superiors, and yet engaged upon a common work in the same place, the more insoluble they seemed.'[53] More importantly, there was the danger that jealousy and competition might develop between the secular clergy and the recently arrived monks. Another problem, specifically Benedictine, also clouded the horizon. All English Benedictine monks took a 'missionary oath,' which bound them to work for the conversion of England to Roman Catholicism. The General Chapter of the Congregation, and not the superiors of individual houses, was the governing body of the English Benedictine Congregation. The Chapter could, for example, transfer a monk from one house to another, or re-assign a monk from parish to parish. 'The monasteries were looked upon as little more than Seminaries in which the monks spent a few years of their life preparing themselves for their *real* work, the apostolic mission.'[54]

The Chapter could, and did, appoint monks throughout the English mission territory at will. Since all English Benedictines were pledged to the missions, 'it was hardly expected that they would acquiesce in any arrangement which might permanently exclude them from missionary work altogether.'[55] To extinguish any rivalry between the secular clergy and the Benedictine monks and to side-step the obstacle of the missionary oath, while retaining the presence of monks, Cardinal Vaughan proposed a solution which caused great consternation among all elements of English Roman Catholicism.

If English Benedictines posed difficulties, why not another congregation of monks? A solution to Vaughan's 'difficulties seemed to have been found when he thought of another Benedictine Congregation which, unlike the English Benedictines, had no missionary character, and so was prepared to devote itself exclusively to a life of prayer and the work of singing the Divine Office.'[56] Long renowned for their liturgical expertise in the rendering of plain chant, the monks of Solesmes appeared to be the perfect candidates, and so Cardinal Vaughan began to negotiate with these French monks.

3. THE SAGA OF THE FRENCH MONKS

If Cardinal Vaughan wanted to grace Westminster Cathedral with beautiful liturgy and music, the accomplishments of Solesmes Abbey in France could not be ignored. Since the middle of the nineteenth century, the Abbaye Saint-Pierre near the village of Solesmes had been recognized as the pioneer in liturgical studies, especially plain chant. Founded as a priory in the eleventh century, Solesmes was destroyed by the English during the Hundred Years' War, only to be rebuilt during the Renaissance. Fuelled by the attacks of the Enlightenment against organized religion, the anticlericalism and secularism generated by the French Revolution naturally attacked the alleged corruption and parasitical lifestyle of the monastic houses. As a consequence of this Solesmes was dissolved, and its monks dispersed throughout the country. In 1833, the local curate, Prosper Gueranger (1805-1875), purchased the monastic property at Solesmes, eventually restored the Benedictine horarium, and was appointed in 1837 its first Abbot by Pope Gregory XVI. Soon afterwards, Rome honoured Solesmes and designated it as the head of a new French congregation of Benedictine monks.

In addition to being a founding father of nineteenth century French monasticism, Gueranger created at Solesmes 'a community whose spiritual life was above all centred in experienced contact with the prayer of the Church.'[1] Moreover, Gueranger rejected some of the French or Gallic forms of worship, and favoured instead the Roman liturgy. Consequently, this signalled

The domes of the cathedral

a renaissance for plain chant insofar as he was 'interested in restoring at Solesmes pure Benedictine practice, including the authentic Gregorian chant.'[2] The proper rendition of chant, therefore, became Guéranger's chief concern.

His methodology and the quality of liturgical music sung at Solesmes soon attracted a following throughout Europe. Guéranger was a 'pioneer in drawing general attention to the beauty of the forms and texts that had been preserved in the Roman liturgy . . . .'[3] His numerous publications, his scholarly research into the history of plain chant and his maxim that one must go back to the original sources, earned both Solesmes and its Abbot an international reputation. Guéranger, therefore, was cast as a liturgical expert of the highest calibre. Vaughan's firsthand experience of the Solesmes liturgy during his European trips had impressed him greatly. Further, Guéranger's exaltation of the Roman liturgy stereotyped him as an Ultramontane, and this also appealed to Vaughan's sensitivities.

The fame of the Solesmes school of liturgical interpretation continued after Guéranger's death. Another monk, Joseph Pothier (1835-1923) continued musical research and published *Les Mélodies grégoriennes d'aprés la tradition* in 1880. Here, 'the laws of oratorical rhythm were better defined and more solidly established, and the role and the nature of the Latin accent brought to light.'[4] His other works, based on ancient manuscripts, resurrected the style and form of the original chant. Throughout the century, therefore, the liturgical method of Solesmes and its interpretation gradually gained an acceptance by the ecclesiastical authorities. But the changing political climate in France did not smile on Solesmes; the government closed the monastery in 1880 and again from 1882 to 1896. For a short period of time. Abbot Paul Delatte (he was Abbot from 1890 to 1920) successfully struggled to restore a monastic routine in the face of French secularism. By bringing a choir of Solesmes monks to England, Vaughan would earn praise as a saviour – as well as a promoter – of their great tradition.

In addition to the sympathy felt towards their co-religious on the Continent, the approval and use of the Solesmes liturgy at Rome also impressed the English Catholics. In 1901, for example, *The Tablet* reported that 'the Holy Father sent a brief of commendation to the Benedictines of Solesmes in recognition of Plain Chant in accordance with ancient tradition.'' In commenting on this papal brief of Leo XIII, the paper noted that 'one thing is certain, that if uniformity is to be secured in the chant of the Church, it will not be realized in the universal adoption of the Ratisbon edition.'⁶ The article continued, 'in Rome itself the Solesmes edition is used in the Vatican Seminary, in the French, Capranican, and the South American Colleges, and in the Benedictine College of St. Anselm's.' In Cardinal Vaughan's mind the services of the Solesmes monks guaranteed excellent liturgical services at Westminster Cathedral, and he urged Abbot Delatte to respond to his offer.

The exact date is not known, but by the early summer of 1899 a preliminary understanding had been reached between Cardinal Vaughan and Abbot Paul Delatte. Vaughan's invitation to Delatte has not survived, so some mystery surrounds its exact contents. It does appear, however, that the English Cardinal only wanted the Solesmes monks on a temporary basis. Delatte's notes support this:

> It seems to me that it is difficult, at the moment when the Cardinal is making such an honourable offer, to foresee the future and even predict the moment when the Abbey of Westminster [West-

51

minster Cathedral!] having been provided with
English personnel . . . the French element shall
be expected to withdraw on its own initiative.[7]

Delatte wanted to avoid any secrecy in his dealings with
Vaughan, and he also understood the Cardinal's desire
for an experimental French foundation in London. 'It
will be the natural thing to give back to the English
Benedictine Congregation a house which rightly belongs to it,' his notes further record, 'and perhaps it
would be preferable to say this openly, and to write it
into the Charter of the Foundation, so that we do not
appear in any way as interlopers or usurpers.'[8] Delatte's
papers reveal that he gave more than cursory attention
to the proposed London scheme; there are references
to a year's trial period (September 1900 to September
1901); the actual construction of a monastery; the
number of monks needed; the endowment required;
and regulations for the monastic life of the French
monks. Before replying to Cardinal Vaughan's offer,
Abbot Delatte confided with and sought the advice of
his friend, Bishop Abel Gilbert.[9]

Delatte had informed Bishop Gilbert of his intended
response to Cardinal Vaughan's proposal. Gilbert replied in a lengthy letter congratulating the Abbot on his
reply to Vaughan. This Bishop, however, was not
reserved, still less an anglophile, and he challenged
Delatte to seize this valuable opportunity:

> The project itself appears to me one of the most
> eminent things a religious family could become
> interested in. In my eyes it is a new invasion of
> England, tottering in its Protestantism, by the
> monks, who re-establish there assuredly and
> with a rapidly-spreading influence, liturgical

The crypt: Cardinal Manning's tomb

CARDINAL·HENRY·EDWARD·MANNING
SECOND ARCHBISHOP OF WESTMINSTER, BORN JULY 15, 1808:
CONSECRATED ARCHBISHOP JUNE 8, 1865: CREATED CARDINAL PRIEST
MARCH 19, 1875. DIED JANUARY 14, 1892, AND BURIED AT KENSAL GREEN.
HIS BODY WAS TRANSLATED TO THIS TOMB JANUARY 25, 1907

> worship in its most exact and most beautiful
> form . . . and scholarly orthodoxy, in a local and
> special form, adjusting slightly, thanks to very
> suitable specialists, to the needs and the defic-
> iencies of Anglican theology . . .[10]

The spirit and character of the Solesmes Congregation
must be safeguarded, and this could be guaranteed by a
firm commitment to a scholarly apostolate.

Bishop Gilbert gently chided Delatte on the Abbot's
acceptance of Cardinal Vaughan's suggestion that the
French foundation should only be temporary. 'What is
needed is not a trial,' he urged, 'but a triumph';
continuing,

> What is necessary is not preliminary steps lead-
> in to a progressive ascent, there is needed
> something substantial from the beginning, which
> compels recognition and inspires respect, cap-
> able even of being lessened later without dimin-
> ishing the results accomplished at a first stroke.
> In fact you have, dear friend, to assert yourself
> in the public opinion from the moment of the
> first contact; to furnish the Cardinal with a
> triumph from the very beginning; not to leave
> any objection that he has to answer; not to leave
> him with a hostile statement that he can shrug
> off with a smile.

The French must, moreover, be independent, and
avoid any co-operation with the English Benedictines!
It was not the presence of a few Britons in the new
monastery that would be objectionable but 'it is the
idea that you need them, that they know it, or would
think so.' 'Guests of yours, that is possible,' Bishop
Gilbert mused, but 'co-founders with you, to me that
seems full of dangers.'[11]

Abbot Delatte's response to Vaughan's invitation,
however, reflected the cautious and prudent approach

of his notes, and rejected the ecclesiastical jingoism of Bishop Gilbert. In general, his lengthy letter was enthusiastic about the prospect of French monks from his monastery being associated with Westminster Cathedral. The Abbot's answer was intended 'to fix the conditions which appear . . . to render possible the foundation of the Abbey of Westminster, and to determine the part to be undertaken by the congregation of Solesmes.'[12] Delatte explained the reasons behind the French eagerness. He did so by appealing to the universal and catholic character of the Roman Church. Abbot Delatte believed that the proposal of the Archbishop 'proves to us that Catholics are united by a tie stronger than that of nationality.'[13] The future of Westminster, however, 'will not be definitely assured until the services of the Archiepiscopal Church have been entrusted to monks taken from British soil.' Delatte strongly rejected in fact Bishop Gilbert's approach; no action or plans could exclude the English Benedictines. 'It is, therefore our duty to tend towards this end and to act, at the moment, in such a way as to ensure for the future what we have foreseen and desired.'[14]

By the turn of the century, Dom Aidan Gasquet (1846-1929) had already been recognised as an eminent historian and a leading authority in questions dealing with English Roman Catholicism.[15] He also enjoyed a reputation throughout European monastic circles as an influential member of the English Benedictines. For these reasons, Abbot Delatte contacted him about the possibility of the Solesmes monks establishing a foundation in London. While a student, young Gasquet believed that he might have a monastic vocation, and in 1866 he entered the Benedictine novitiate at Belmont. A year later, Dom Aidan returned to Downside to teach. He was ordained a priest in 1874 and soon took charge of the studies at the school where a contemporary described him as 'revelling in work' and 'eaten up with activity.'[16] In 1878, he became Prior at Downside, a post he held for nearly seven years. During his term of office, the abbey church was enlarged and the school modernized, and his friendship with the medievalist and liturgist, Edmund Bishop, helped shape the young Prior's future vocation as an historian. Overwork and exhaustion contributed to heart problems, and this eventually forced Gasquet to resign the office of Prior, in the summer of 1885.

From Downside, he went to London for a period of recuperation, but at the same time he also started to study British history, and began to research at the British Museum. The times were encouraging for ecclesiastical historians: Leo XIII had recently opened the Vatican archives to serious scholars, and encouraged clergymen to devote themselves to a career in church history. Supported in his new academic vocation by Cardinal Manning, Gasquet was allowed to stay in London and continue his work. The British Museum and the Public Record Office supplied the material for Gasquet's two-volume work, *Henry VIII and the English Monasteries*, published in 1888 and 1889 respectively. These books, which seriously questioned the traditional Protestant view of the Reformation, were well-received, and Gasquet soon found himself fêted as an accomplished historian, although David Knowles has expressed serious reservations about Gasquet's originality as a thinker.[17] Knowles also pointed out Gasquet's frequent inaccuracies and remarked that 'one or two of his later compositions gave one the mental impression of being lost in a maze or engulfed in a nightmare.'[18] More importantly, Professor Knowles believed that 'there was a root of something in Gasquet which led him to ignore even the most cogent evidence against anything he had written.' Despite these shortcomings, Aidan Gasquet's works, especially those dealing with the history of *The Book of Common Prayer*, caught the eye of Rome. The question of the validity of Anglican Orders had again surfaced.

With his historian's credentials and his knowledge of the Tudor era, Gasquet seemed a natural choice to join his fellow Englishmen, Mgr J Moyes and Fr D Fleming, as a member of Leo XIII's international commission of 1896 to reconsider the Anglican claims. The work of the commission and the condemnation of Anglican Orders in the *Apostolicae Curae* (1896) brought him international status, but the trip to Rome also introduced him to Merry del Val, the future Secretary of State, and Pope Leo XIII. In 1899, Leo XIII commissioned Gasquet with the task of carrying out the reform of the English Benedictine Congregation.[19] This was the churchman – later to be President of the English Benedictine Congregation in 1900, a possible successor to Cardinal Vaughan in 1903, commissioned to revise the *Vulgate* in 1907, and created a Cardinal in 1914 – whom Abbot Delatte approached in 1899.

Abbot Delatte argued that he must meet with Aidan Gasquet,[20] and acquaint him 'with the terms upon which the French Colony of Monks are to take up their position.'[21] 'They are brothers in religion,' he asserted, 'and such a course of action would be both right and equitable.'[22] In spite of their missionary character, the duties associated with Westminster Cathedral must eventually be transferred to the English monks, yet the French monks 'would be allowed to put forward their claim for definitely remaining in England.'[23]

Delatte had originally contemplated a trial period of one year for his monks in London, but Bishop Gilbert's insistence on a longer time-span triumphed. Vaughan's proposed year, September 1900 to September 1901, was insufficient, and Delatte urged a three-year period with 'the understanding that they [the French monks] will be there to render service.'[24] If the time came when his monks were no longer needed by the Archbishop, Delatte agreed to withdraw them from Westminster: 'I am certainly of opinion that the only grounds upon which we can lay a solid foundation for establishing our Religious in Westminster are those of perfect freedom for both parties.'[25]

Abbot Delatte worked for a spirit of compromise, but had no doubt that the French monks would not only remain, but prosper in central London. He even approached Vaughan about the specifications of the future monastic buildings. In the summer of 1899, he informed the Cardinal, '. . . the plan of the monastery which is to be founded and built . . . [should] be prepared by a monk.'[26] The monastery would contain rooms for thirty French monks, a refectory, cloister, and Chapter House. Individuals wanting to make a retreat would also be received. Delatte argued that the Solesmes Congregation must still retain control over St. Michael's Abbey at Farnborough,[27] 'for the health of the monks would certainly suffer from being constantly detained without any relaxation in the centre of a large city like London.'[28]

The Abbey of Solesmes, however, could not promise a full contingent of French monks: 'I can only place at Your Eminence's disposal the Fathers of the community of St. Michael to which I will add three or four monks taken from Solesmes.'[29] The English Benedictines must augment the French. 'If the Anglo-Benedictine Congregation will consent to supply four or five subjects,' Delatte believed, 'this will bring the figures up to

Chapel of St Thomas of Canterbury: the Vaughan chantry

about twenty for the first or trial year, 1900-1901.'[30] Payment, immediate housing, and pastoral duties could be discussed at a future date. Chanting the Divine Office would be the important responsibility of the Solesmes monks. Abbot Delatte briefly mentioned plans for a monastic library, and drew attention to Vaughan's desire to build one, which was 'to be entrusted to the care of one of the monks.'[31] In conclusion, the Abbot forecast the sensitive and emotional difficulties facing French monks at Westminster. 'However, the most difficult problem of all will be that of arranging a *modus vivendi* between the regular secular clergy in the Cathedral where the Monks, the Chapter and the parish priests will be thrown together.'[32]

Cardinal Vaughan immediately sought the counsel and advice of Mgr Moyes, Canon of the cathedral, who in turn prepared for the Cardinal two documents: a précis of Abbot Delatte's letter of 11 June 1899, and a list of stipulations based on the Delatte letter modified with the necessary explanation for any change. In a covering letter, Mgr Moyes stated that other questions needed to be addressed, for example, the horarium, charges for maintenance, use of the sanctuary, but these could wait. In Moyes' point of view,

> the coming of the monks is doubly important, not only to furnish the basis of the plain-chant and secure the ideal of the Liturgical Office (which ought to be independent of any consideration of the attendance of the people) but as planting in our midst a permanent body of spiritual and learned men who will think, and study and write in all those departments of research which affect intellectually the conversion of England.[33]

Moyes argued that their 'spiritual life would be to us a constant guarantee of their humility, orthodoxy, and loyalty of spirit, such as we cannot easily have with mere student units.'[34]

Moyes' abstract of Delatte's letter emphasized the vague wording of the Abbot's proposals. He drew attention to the fact that 'the agreement between the Cardinal and the Abbot is based on the condition that the position of the monks at the Cathedral shall rest upon a title which is purely precarious . . .'[35] Moyes contended that in any agreement 'it ought to be stated that the authority to be satisfied on this important point is the Archbishop.'[36] In respect of the three-year trial period, he believed that this was desirable and that 'nothing of the nature of a contract or binding agreement of any kind be contemplated: better still if 'the period of experiment becomes continual and the monks remain while the Archbishop is satisfied with the working.'[37] Delatte favoured a monastery to house his monks immediately, but Moyes believed this would 'seem to commit the See to a permanent Monastic connection before the period had elapsed.'[38] Consequently, he advised Vaughan to avoid setting a date for the construction of a monastery and that special care 'should be taken that nothing on the part of the monks of Solesmes be allowed by which a vested interest be created in favour of the monks on the soil of Westminster Cathedral.'[39]

Moyes also detailed his thoughts on the possible liturgical duties of the Solesmes monks. He revealed a fear that they might become permanently entrenched at Westminster Cathedral. In respect of the Divine Office, Mgr Moyes suggested that the monks 'ought not to have the right to the choir, [as Delatte had suggested] but to the use of the choir during the hours of liturgical service.'[40] In other words, the stalls would be reserved for the monks but should not be considered as their exclusive and private property. The schedule of services should be the subject of future discussions between the monastic and parochial superiors and subject to the approval of the Archbishop. In no way, however, should the Divine Office take precedence over any parish or congregational function. In his letter to Vaughan, the Abbot of Solesmes had insisted that his monks, in addition to singing, be entrusted with the maintenance of order in the church, its cleaning, and 'the heating of the Cathedral.' Again Moyes sought to limit the power and authority of these French monks. 'The first alone of these — the singing of plain-chant,' he suggested, 'properly belongs to the monks.' 'The remaining three . . . ought to be done under the authority and direction of the Cathedral Administration or a Committee appointed by the Archbishop. . .'[41] Moyes suggested that marriages, baptisms, burials and their respective fees remain a 'matter for arrangement between the Archbishop and his parochial Administrator.'[42] Even the proposed library must not be handed over to the monks; it must be archiepiscopal, not monastic. A librarian, who was not a Benedictine, would supervise its operation.

Incorporating the above suggestions and amendments, Monsignor Moyes composed a new agreement.[43] This document, *Preliminary Articles of Agreement*, was sent to Cardinal Vaughan to serve as the basis for continued talks with the French. According to this proposal, the monks of Solesmes would be a valuable addition to the fabric of the cathedral, but under no circumstance should they be extended a *carte blanche*. Moyes also informed the Cardinal that trouble might plague his plan to import the French. He warned that

Early view of the font showing unclad walls

'in a Cathedral in which the Ordinary, the Chapter, and the monks and the Parish priest or parochial Administrator tread on the same ground there will be a certain measure of complex working.'[44] Mgr Moyes suggested the creation of a permanent committee consisting of all concerned parties to work out any future difficulties. He prized the contribution the Solesmes monks would make to Westminster Cathedral, but he emphasized that control must not pass from the Archbishop. Moyes concluded his letter to Cardinal Vaughan with the following advice: 'I hope for the good of the Church in England, Your Eminence will press forward with a strong hand.'[45]

By the summer of 1899, therefore, Cardinal Vaughan had already won pledges of support and commitment from two Benedictine Congregations. But the flow of financial contributions for the construction of his dream cathedral dried to a trickle. Vaughan was forced to remind the faithful of their responsibilities, and the pages of *The Tablet* became his platform. One article, 'Our Catholic Opportunity,' pointed out to its readers that a revival in English Roman Catholicism was flourishing, and on the other hand, a growing reaction against Anglican practices was evident. 'To all who keep watchful eyes upon the religious signs of the times,' *The Tablet* recorded, 'nothing can be more certain that a large, an influential, and a daily increasing section of the English people is undergoing a reaction from the beliefs, the methods, and the spirit of the Protestant Reformation.'[46] The Reformers 'introduced doctrinal poverty and called it Evangelical purity. They imposed liturgical baldness and called it Evangelical simplicity.' The English mind and spirit, however, could not tolerate such aberrations: 'The religious life of a great and generous people could not be forever cramped within such starved and pitiable ideals.'[47] Part of the mission of the new cathedral would be to bring these questioning Anglicans into the fold of Peter:

> Then just as the English People are moving away in disillusionment from the ideals of the Reformation, and are becoming more and more earnest in their cry for that which is beautiful and stately in worship, so there exists for the Catholic Church in this country a duty to meet it, and to prove that she alone possesses, and that she alone can give, in all its truth and fullness, that for which the souls of this land are seeking, and for which so many have happily learned to hunger.[48]

Vaughan claimed that an ornate building complete with 'the beauty and completeness of the Catholic Liturgy in all its wondrous power...' would quickly draw converts. Consequently, it was imperative that English Roman Catholics continue to contribute: 'Its success in this high mission will be what the Catholics of this land make it.'[49]

During the spring, Cardinal Vaughan used the columns of *The Tablet* to keep English Roman Catholics informed of the construction of their cathedral. In one account, the writer described in detail the construction of the building, and even implied that the new church might rival St Paul's. Still money was urgently needed. Cash donations since June 1894 had amounted to over £100,000, but the article warned: 'still it is necessary to point out that if the Cathedral is to be solemnly opened in September, 1900, more money is wanted and wanted quickly.'[50] In the June edition it was noted that some progress had been made. Work on the choir-stalls for the monks, for example, had been completed. However, Catholics were urged to continue their generosity: 'Surely the devotion of the English people to the Holy

See should of itself enable funds to be raised sufficient to complete the carcase of St. Peter's Chapel.'[51]

Cardinal Vaughan believed that Westminster Cathedral would shine as an example of the piety of English Catholics, and would draw some Anglicans out of their liturgical malaise, leading them to the splendours of Roman Catholicism. He touched on another emotion: an appeal to patriotism – illogical in light of the Cardinal's negotiations with the French monks! – was the theme of a pastoral letter from Archbishop's House. The pages of *The Tablet*, *The Times*, and *The Weekly Register* printed Vaughan's challenge to the laity for contributions to their new church, which 'will be not only the Mother Church of the principal English diocese, but the Metropolitan Church of the Province of Westminster.'[52] The pastoral emphasized the themes of patriotism and chauvinism. 'The truth is,' the Cardinal pleaded, 'that the Westminster Cathedral must be. . . much more than the chief church of a diocese . . . London is the capital of the British Empire, and the highest city of the world.' London represented the 'centre of British power, British policy, and British wealth.' Westminster Cathedral, therefore, embodied the greatness of London and Great Britain. Vaughan believed that 'every member of every flock in this country has an interest in this House of the Lord which zealous and brave hearts are endeavouring to set up in Westminster, near the ancient shrine of the old religion of the land.'[53] Westminster Cathedral, therefore, captured the magic of England's past, represented the spirit of the present generation, and pointed toward the future greatness of the country's Roman Catholics. In light of this, Cardinal Vaughan's invitation to the Solesmes monks seemed incongruous to many English.

4. THE MONKS VERSUS THE SECULAR CLERGY

The year 1899 witnessed a revolution in the philosophy and character of the English Benedictine Congregation. An editorial in *The Weekly Register* reported that the priories of Ampleforth, Douai, and Downside had been raised to the dignity of abbeys through the action of the Holy See. The article declared that the history of the English Benedictine Congregation was 'intimately bound up with the Catholic Church in England in a way which is peculiar to itself;'[1] that 'No Religious Order is so thoroughly English as the Benedictine; it appeals to the English taste and the English character as no other ever has.' It must be 'the fact that the English Benedictines are representatives of the ancient Abbey of Westminster,' and the article concluded, 'that such perceptions led Cardinal Vaughan to form the intention – which he had publicly announced on more than one occasion – of attaching them to the new cathedral.'[2] *The Catholic Times and Catholic Opinion* also rejoiced in the new honours bestowed on the English Benedictines. 'What Catholic can forget all that the Fathers of St Benedict did for religion in the dark days of persecution? What Catholic forgets the noble and self-sacrificing labours of St Benedict's cowled sons up and down the length and breadth of England to-day?'[3] The present, according to many English Catholics, would be the fitting time to install these English monks in the new Westminster Cathedral.

The change referred to in the press constituted a substantial revolution in the governance and direction[4] of the English Benedictines: the missionary character was altered in favour of a more traditional Benedictine and monastic flavour. Edmund Ford, the Prior of Downside, claimed that 'with the growth in the number of the secular clergy, the assistance of the monks on the parishes was not of such paramount importance and that the monastic life should again become the predominant factor in English Benedictine polity.'[5] Ford argued that the 'English Benedictines had for many decades lived under a *lex particularis*, especially formed to meet abnormal circumstances which had long ceased to operate, and the continuance of such a system was unreasonable and illogical.'[6] This emphasis on the monastic as opposed to a parochial character was opposed by a majority of the English Benedictine Congregation, and it took the personal intervention of Pope Leo XIII in 1899 to settle the so-called 'constitutional crisis.'

The Pope issued a bull, *Diu Quidem*, which effectively transformed the constitutions of the English Benedictine Congregation. In the first place, *Diu Quidem* raised the Benedictine priories to abbeys. Recognising that 'there is a danger lest such divergence of opinion... should occasion a loss of mutual charity,' *Dui Quidem* stated the following:

> Judging then that these evils should be prevented, we have taken the whole matter again into our own hands: and we will and prescribe that in compiling the Constitutions of the English Benedictine Congregation the following enactments be inserted, to be always and inviolably observed.[7]

The first 'enactment' was the establishment of independent abbeys which enjoyed all the traditional privileges and authority and autonomy.[8] *Diu Quidem* also commanded the English Benedictines to observe a series of earlier legislative principles embodied in the bull *Religiosus Ordo* (1890).

Columns of the sanctuary

Cardinal Vaughan contacted the Solesmes monks because of the loose administration of the English Congregation and their devotion to missionary travels. *Diu Quidem* rectified this. Vaughan also worried about the possible instability of the English monks if stationed at Westminster because of their missionary oath. The bull *Religiosus Ordo* addressed this concern. This document reasserted and emphasised the monastic character of life for the English Benedictines. The bull succinctly addressed the problems:

> At the present moment matters have come to such a pass, that the very peace of the body is in danger: for there are some who call in question whether the English Benedictine Congregation is in its essence and nature monastic or missionary: and again whether the supreme authority belongs to the monasteries, and the missions ought therefore to be subject to the monasteries; or whether the missions are free to carry on their work by their own laws, and are exempt from all obedience to the monasteries.[9]

'Now it is perfectly clear,' it continued, 'that the English Benedictine Congregation is by its very nature monastic.'[10] A sense of permanence, structure, and stability was introduced into the English Benedictine Congregation. What Cardinal Vaughan feared most had been rectified by the actions of the Vatican. But he had already approached the French! He was now in the unenviable position of having offered the same position to two different groups of monks. Moreover, Cardinal Vaughan did not expect opposition from members of his flock to the Solesmes scheme. The revelation that French monks might replace the English Benedictines was greeted with patriotic shock.

The 15 July 1899 edition of *The Weekly Register* reported that it was 'surprised that we do not hear from

England any comment upon another arrangement, *viz* that the Cardinal Archbishop has arranged to put his new Cathedral at Westminster into the hands, not of the English Benedictines . . . but of the Benedictines of Solesmes.'[11] The paper stated that 'this was a step of very doubtful expediency, and not likely to conduce to harmony in England.'[12] A week later, the same paper told its readers that there was strong opposition to this plan from the Cathedral Chapter of Westminster, and consequently this might jeopardize Cardinal Vaughan's plan to introduce the French monks into London: 'At any rate, it relieves us, for the present, from the necessity of commenting on the proposed introduction of foreigners into the English Cathedral.'[13] The report pointed out that a financial drive for the Cathedral had recently been launched, and 'that appeal would be greatly assisted by an assurance that the Cathedral will be national and English in fact as well as in name.'[14] But the paper was soon forced to admit that its confidence that the French scheme would be abandoned was premature.

The title of the next editorial, 'A New Alien Priory,' captured the indignation of the paper. The Cathedral Chapter, according to this report, opposed the Cardinal's wishes, and therefore

> it would be an act of cowardice on our part if we failed to assure the members of the Chapter that they will have the support of the great majority of the Catholic clergy and laity of England in resisting an arrangement which would be one of the greatest blunders that has yet been committed in the adminstration of the English Church.[15]

The editorial claimed that 'the rank and file of Catholics have a right to be heard.' That 'clergy and laity are not dumb driven cattle, and when they see that there is imminent danger of a false step being taken which will injure the Church and put back her advance, they will be wanting in their duty if they did not at least remonstrate.'

With a touch of irony, the paper commented that when it first heard the rumours of the invitation of the French monks to Westminster Cathedral, 'we regarded the story as the invention of an enemy.' It continued, 'The report seemed so wildly improbable that we hesitated to credit it.' So appeals to patriotism strengthened the case against the French: 'It is bad enough to have any foreigner forced upon us,' the paper quipped, 'we have only to imagine the effect on the English mind of a national English cathedral with forty Frenchmen piping the office in an apse behind the high altar.' Any non-English element detracted from the dignity of Westminster, but 'France, of all the countries in the world just at the present time, is chosen as the country from which they are to be imported.'[16]

Not all English Roman Catholics sympathized with the objections raised by the editorials in *The Weekly Register*. One of its readers did hope that the article 'had its desired effect, and put an end to the project of having the Cathedral of Westminster served by foreigners.'[17] Economics and the extent of French power were the questions raised by this weak protest. But many Catholics supported Cardinal Vaughan. *The Catholic Times and Catholic Opinion* told its readers that 'the Cardinal may be trusted to have acted for the best' by negotiating to bring the Solesmes monks to Westminster.[18] No doubt, the article continued, 'only the most weighty reasons have impelled him to select the Benedictine Fathers of Solesmes for the performance

Saint George's chapel

of the sacred functions to which their lives will be devoted.' It noted that 'the Church in this country will be enriched by the presence of one more of the religious Orders which adorn while they serve the Kingdom of God on earth.' The paper urged people of all classes to give the French a traditional warm English welcome. As for the English monks, the article concluded:

> It would have been a thousand pities to take away any of the English Benedictines from the work which in missions and colleges they have for so long and with such steadiness and ability performed for the church in this land.[19]

Those who supported the Cardinal, however, did not avoid the questions of the English Benedictines or patriotism. 'If he elects to secure the services of the English Benedictines we shall all rejoice,' but '. . . we should lament the loss of their invaluable services from mission and school.'[20] In response to such cries as 'foreigners' and 'the invasion of foreign monks,' the paper retorted, 'We have no more dread of an invasion of foreign monks than we have of an invasion of Chinese Black Flags.' If the Solesmes monks chant the Divine Office, 'we shall still sleep quite calmly, as little terrified at the prospect [as] of the invasion of Polar bears.' Gone are the days when outsiders can harm the British character, 'the English people can afford to be large minded in these matters.'[21] The edition for 25 August pleaded that 'more than one Benedictine monastery might conceivably exist in the city of Westminster.'[22] The author also posed an interesting solution to the problem: permit the Solesmes monks to serve the new Westminster Cathedral; but 'so long as the Ampleforth Community continues there will be no other legitimate representative of St. Peter's Abbey, Westminster.'[23]

Even readers of *The Weekly Register* attacked the paper's harsh treatment of the French monks. One correspondent, for example, accused the paper of manufacturing an argument which seemed 'as if it had come straight out of any Protestant History of England.'[24] This writer scorned its attitude and reminded the editor that 'we do not wish to adopt the early anticipations of Protestantism which produced the Statutes of Praemunire and Provisors.' 'Theodore, Lanfranc, Anselm, are names of foreigners,' the article continued, and 'a foreigner received John Henry Newman into the Church.' The main argument in favour of Cardinal Vaughan's plan, however, was the catholicity of the Roman Church. 'The Church is Catholic, and when once the principle of nationality is admitted you historically approach schism, you come to Orthodox Russia and Protestant England.'[25]

If the laity and Catholic press approached the question of the French monks from different viewpoints, the mind of the secular clergy was also far from unified. From the beginning of the controversy, the focus was on what action the Cathedral Chapter would take.[26] The viewpoint of the Chapter remained clouded, but it appears that they expressed 'strenuous opposition' to the presence of the Solesmes monks at Westminster.[27] *The Weekly Register* reported that the Chapter viewed Vaughan's proposal with disfavour, which was 'practically unanimous,' but by the end of July 1899 it had 'not yet arrived at a formal decision.'[28] At the July Chapter meeting, presided over by Vaughan, the Cardinal placed before it 'his plan concerning the ritual and choral arrangements for the new Cathedral' and read the letter from Abbot Delatte which outlined the French conditions.[29] Vaughan then tried to calm any fears. He insisted that 'no binding agreement should be made between the parties' until four years had elapsed.

Moreover, the Solesmes Benedictines would not usurp the duties of the secular clergy. According to Vaughan, 'the monks would be responsible merely for the conduct of the daily Cathedral Service – High Mass and Vespers.' 'They would neither preach nor hear confessions. Being strictly cenobites, they would confine themselves to prayer and study.' The official record expressed a benign consensus and 'after further conversation, the subject was closed.'[30] *The Weekly Register* continued to assure the Canons, however, that they could count on the support of loyal Roman Catholics in resisting the presence of the French monks in London. While the press argued the merits of the Solesmes scheme, and while the Chapter debated what course of action it would take, a pamphlet appeared which proposed that the secular clergy exclusively should run and administer Westminster Cathedral.

Written by Ethelred L. Taunton,[31] *A Letter to His Eminence Herbert Cardinal Vaughan Archbishop of Westminster on the Work of the Clergy at the Westminster Cathedral* championed the rights and privileges of the secular clergy at the new Cathedral. The author praised Vaughan for his dedicated work 'of raising the clergy to their rightful place in the English Church.'[32] The English clergy, Fr Taunton maintained, '... want opportunities; they want to be called upon to *do* something.' As for members of religious orders, 'the monastic Order is not opposed to the Clerical Order ... It runs along side of it, keeps it, and sustains it in the divinely appointed work.'[33] His objective was not to compare, to praise, or to criticize, but to argue for the rightful place of the secular clergy at Westminster Cathedral. 'The clergy can do the work of the cathedral: they can be made to do the work as efficiently as anyone else.' 'The new Cathedral,' he maintained, 'will be an object lesson to the whole of England.' His position was strong and forceful:

> Who, then, so fit to do the Church's work as the
> Sons of the Diocese? Who so capable as those
> who, by divine institutions are servants of the
> Sanctuary? Let your Clergy have this opport-
> unity, let them be called upon to do the liturgical
> work; and I will warrant your Eminence will
> have reason, and good reason, to be proud of
> your own sons.[34]

Benedictines in charge of the Cathedral's liturgy, whether French or English, insulted the secular clergy. 'But we shall never get any real Liturgical progress amongst us,' he pleaded with Cardinal Vaughan, until 'the Clergy *do* the Liturgy themselves and inspire a love for it in others.'[35] Public worship at Westminster must be an example to all English Catholics, and it must reflect the spirit and personality of the nation: 'Osten-tatious pageantry, tickling of ears, attracting crowds to hear some singers are not your Eminence's objects.' Taunton suggested the following: 'a small College of six Priests, with a Canon in residence, to represent the Chapter,'[36] and choir-school would supply trained voices for the future.

Fr Taunton not only opposed the invitation to the Benedictines, but also mocked the style of music perfected by the Solesmes monks. Plain chant, he maintained, 'ought to be the foundation of every Ecclesiastical Choir School,' but not the tradition of the Solesmes monks. The style found 'in the manuscript by the Solesmes editors is not in any way representative of the pure Roman Type.' He also appealed to the nationalism of the English Catholics in rejecting this French interpretation: 'I have more than a suspicion that future research . . . will show that the true source of the Solesmes Chant is Gallican, not Roman.'[37] In conclusion, Fr Taunton believed that 'there is a most happy opportunity of carrying on your Eminence's desire to help the clergy to their rightful position by making them do a work which is theirs by every claim.'[38]

Despite some isolated protests and objections against the settlement of French monks at Westminster Cathedral, Cardinal Vaughan could still count on the support of some English Roman Catholics. Letters to the Catholic press and editorials expressed unquestioned loyalty to the will of the Cardinal Archbishop. The threat of open rebellion on the part of the Cathedral Chapter failed to materialize; throughout the summer this body vacillated and failed to reach a consensus. Consequently, Cardinal Vaughan continued to hope for a successful outcome of his desire to install a choir of French monks in London. In June 1899, he even visited the Abbey of Solesmes to meet with Abbot Delatte about his project,[39] but no evidence survives which sheds light on this meeting. Nonetheless, this visit must have raised the expectations of the French. Fr Ferdinand Cabrol, the French superior of Farnborough Abbey, emerged as an instrumental person in these discussions.

In July 1899, Cabrol expressed both caution and a contempt for the English monks. 'You have heard the news about the [English] Benedictine Congregation,' he wrote Delatte, 'they have abbots now ... I doubt whether they will save them.'[40] He correctly believed that resistance on the part of the English Benedictines to the arrival of the French in London had halted the negotiations. Cabrol warned the Abbot not to trust or co-operate with the English: 'Had we put the Cathedral

The eighth station of the Cross

on a good footing, they would come to take it over.' He used examples from contemporary Anglo-French foreign policy disagreements to illustrate his point.

> Let us not be too generous with them. It's always the same old story. We shriek like badgers because they occupy Egypt, and we are the ones who gave it to them! Let us not make another Egypt for their advantage. It seems to me that this is the lesson for now.[41]

But in spite of this prejudice, Cabrol continued to function as an intermediary between Vaughan and Delatte.

In early August, he told Cardinal Vaughan that Abbot Delatte was still keen about the possibility of a London foundation. Aware of some criticism in England, Delatte was 'not worried about it,' and Cabrol confessed that this 'little press rumour leaves us unconcerned.'[42] What did concern the Solesmes officials was the threatened opposition of the Chapter, who allegedly wanted to 'prevent this foundation or reduce the role of the monks to insignificance.' Cabrol confessed to Vaughan that he had information that the Cathedral Chapter 'will never accept that this monastery becomes an abbey with a Benedictine Abbot who would be endowed with all the rights of his title.' Consequently, 'I do not see how we could accept this monastery if the right to make it an abbey were refused.' Fr Cabrol expressed a wish to continue communications with Cardinal Vaughan, and concluded with an example of historical irony:

> This opposition of a few English Catholics reminds me of Charlemagne, the Great Charlemagne, who, in order to raise the standards of the Gauls, went to seek teachers like Alcuin and other great Englishmen in England, to put them at the head of our schools. France felt honoured

and had applauded these men. What does *The Weekly Register* think about that?[43]

Vaughan replied by addressing the attack in *The Weekly Register* and expressing the hope that neither he nor the Abbot 'will be troubled by it, or by anything else that may be said.'[44] He promised to 'speak when the time comes in a way that will more than vindicate the honour of Solesmes.' The French must be patient: 'A reaction will certainly come about – and we can all afford to wait a little.'[45]

Cabrol assured Delatte that Vaughan was 'truly good, and whatever happens, he will have shown himself a friend toward us.'[46] Cabrol admitted the existence of a press campaign against Solesmes, but maintained that it was 'a staged disturbance.' Vaughan's advisors were questioning his policy and for this reason, Cabrol urged Delatte 'to take a very clear position, and show him that we are ready to do anything to oblige him.'[47] At the end of August, Fr Cabrol informed the Abbot that Cardinal Vaughan still wanted monks from Solesmes, but that the opposition in England still remained intransigent: '. . . the Cardinal is desirous of having us, but is [he] strong enough to impose his will on his Chapter, and to give us the appropriate conditions and guarantees?' He again urged caution, and suggested that in 'these circumstances there is nothing to do but wait . . .'[48]

Cardinal Vaughan faced a more serious problem. What about the monks of the English Congregation whom he had originally invited to settle in London and to conduct the liturgy at his new cathedral? Moreover, the early correspondence and negotiations with the Solesmes monks was carried out without the knowledge of the English Benedictines. The 'Constitutional Crisis' had removed one of Vaughan's original reservations about the Downside monks. A group of English Benedictines had arrived in the London area; land had been purchased in the suburb of Ealing, and construction of a church had begun. During the summer of 1900, Cardinal Vaughan had to inform officials of the English Congregation that he had approached and asked the French to assume those responsibilities already promised to them. The Cardinal not only acted out of politeness; he was forced to admit his action, for the Abbot of Solesmes had made it clear to Vaughan that his monks would come to London only if the co-operation of the English Benedictines was assured. So Cardinal Vaughan sheepishly inquired whether the English monks would relinquish their promised position at Westminster Cathedral and assist the French in conducting the liturgical services.

5. CARDINAL VAUGHAN, THE BENEDICTINES AND THE FRENCH MONKS

Cardinal Vaughan wrote to the President of the English Benedictine Congregation in November 1900 – over a year after he began talks which settled the preliminaries with the French monks. Lack of concern or interest on the part of the English Benedictines is difficult to explain, although one factor might have been that the recent canonical and administrative changes imposed by the Vatican consumed the time and energy of the English superiors.[1] Nevertheless, on 27 November 1900, Cardinal Vaughan wrote to Abbot Gasquet, recently elected President of the English Congregation, inviting him to come to London for 'a good quiet talk with me.'[2] The Cardinal suggested that they dine alone, and devote two or three hours to serious conversation in the afternoon. On 28 November, Abbot Gasquet paid the Cardinal a visit, which lasted several hours. According to Gasquet's notes, 'the most important matter discussed, however, was concerning the Cathedral.'[3] Both parties agreed to speak openly and frankly; Gasquet's interpretation was that 'the whole thing may be put in the proverbial nut-shell.'

> He wants office said in the W[estminster] Cathedral; but 'the Canons' (he said) and many of the clergy desire that the monks be absolutely confined to the singing of the office and have nothing to do in the church.

By this innocent remark Vaughan broached the sensitive issue: the establishment of the Solesmes Benedictines at Westminster. Vaughan struggled to explain why he now desired the French instead of the English Congregation. 'He could not ask us, or indeed any English to undertake to be mere hired choir men,' Gasquet noted, 'and looked around and found the Solesmes monks willing to take the position.' Vaughan tried to calm Gasquet's visible irritation by indicating that he would make no agreement with the French monks independent of the English. According to Abbot Gasquet, 'he was unwilling to come to terms with them (wh[ich] he had not done as yet) without telling us and asking us to approve their coming.'[4]

In addition to this surprise, Gasquet was indignant at the Cardinal's flippant request. What about the previous agreement with the English Congregation? What about the money expended, and the people already committed to the Ealing mission? In addition to these queries, the suggestion that a French congregation replace his own upset the Abbot President. He recorded that 'I pointed out the grave difficulty and the reflection . . . upon us in the public mind.'[5] A 'public insult' was Gasquet's precise choice of words. Moreover, he could 'not conceive how the French O.S.B. could have for a moment entertained the scheme of coming into our province – it was in direct contradiction of our privileges.' The English Abbot asked to see a copy of Abbot Delatte's letter which contained his proposals and conditions for sending French monks to Westminster.[6] He informed the Cardinal that the English Congregation would hold a chapter in February 1901. Gasquet suggested that Vaughan compose a letter which dealt with the Westminster question, promising that he would present the entire matter before the monks at that meeting. Abbot Gasquet ended his recollection of this interview with two questions: 'Why does the Card[inal] want us to say we will agree to the French coming; and he does not generally consider the feelings

A street procession (1908)

of other people . . . there must be some reason, but what?'[7]

On 20 December, the Duke of Norfolk invited Aidan Gasquet to breakfast at Norfolk House. Afterwards, the Duke asked him what he thought about the possibility of the French Benedictines coming to Westminster Cathedral to take charge of the liturgy. The Abbot promised to be candid and informed the Duke 'that it was most objectionable in itself . . . and must inextricably be construed into a distinct insult to us English O.S.B.' Norfolk thanked Abbot Gasquet for his remarks, and confided that Cardinal Vaughan had already spoken to him about the matter. The Duke informed Gasquet that he told Vaughan 'he would have no part in bringing a body of French O.S.B. into London unless it was clearly understood that their English Brethren were quite satisfied.' 'We Catholics,' he concluded, 'have had enough of these misunderstandings . . . .' His meeting with the Duke of Norfolk made it clear to Gasquet that Cardinal Vaughan was serious about bringing the Solesmes Benedictines to London.

Vaughan had himself tried to enlist the support and backing of influential Roman Catholics, like the Duke of Norfolk, for his plan. It appeared, however, that it depended on the support of the English Benedictines. Without it, the Cardinal could not count on the backing of English Catholics. 'This explains,' Gasquet remarked,' why the Cardinal wants us to say we will agree.'[8] Clearly, Cardinal Vaughan had given up on the idea of the English Congregation being associated with the liturgy at Westminster Cathedral. But on the other hand, he urged members of the English Catholic Church to welcome the French monks of Solesmes instead. If the English Benedictines raised a storm of protest, or if they refused to co-operate with the

French, Vaughan's dream would never materialize. Since it appeared that the liturgical duties would not be offered to his congregation of monks as agreed earlier, Abbot Gasquet worked to ensure that the French would never enjoy the prestige of conducting the services in Westminster Cathedral. He faced strong opposition to this plan of scuttling French hopes.

The Tablet continued to print laudatory articles concerning France, its special relationship with Catholic England, and the common bond which united the faithful of the two nations. In an essay entitled 'France and the Conversion of England', one author described the goals of the priests of the French order of St Sulpice as: 'To organize, promote, and foster throughout the whole Christian world a Crusade of Prayer for the return of England to the one True Fold.'[9] Unity of purpose and spirit, therefore, transcended the English Channel. The author also described the relationship between French and English Roman Catholics as a '. . . Holy Alliance held out to us, the spiritual partnership offered to us . . . ' Moreover, the English must co-operate and not compete with their French co-religious: 'We can at least be something more than an approving spectator and a sleeping partner.' The article concluded with a quote from Cardinal Vaughan which emphasized the 'services of charity rendered by the glorious Church of France to the Church of England' begun in 429 AD when Pope Celestinus sent St Germain of Auxerre to England to extinguish the Pelagian heresy.[10]

In November 1900 *The Tablet* printed a report from the Anglican paper *The Church Times*, which described a visit to the Abbey of Solesmes. *The Tablet*, usually scornful of Anglo-Catholic principles and liturgy, published this Anglican essay in praise of the French community. The connection of the French monastery with plain chant was emphasized. 'Solesmes, in fact, is the starting point, the centre of a remarkable liturgical and musical revival in the Latin Church, which is making itself distinctly felt in all quarters of the globe.'[11] In virtual challenge to English Roman Catholics, the author noted that 'we of the Church of England owe a debt of gratitude to Solesmes for having given us a fresh impulse in the correct revival of plain chant.' The article praised every aspect of the French abbey from the architecture to the smallest detail of the daily worship of the monks. The liturgy, naturally, was singled out for admiration:

> You cannot leave Solesmes without a feeling of regret, but there is, at the same time, thankfulness that once in your life, you have been privileged to hear and see the inspired worship of Benedictine monks and nuns, who have restored to the Church that precious heritage of the ages, the plain chant.[12]

Newspaper reports and essays in the Roman Catholic press, however, were not enough to frustrate the opposition of Aidan Gasquet to a Solesmes foundation at Westminster Cathedral.

By the end of 1900 Abbot Gasquet still did not know the details or the extent of the arrangements between Cardinal Vaughan and Abbot Delatte. Gasquet's understanding of the situation was admittedly sketchy: the English monks were to be supplanted at Westminster by the monks of Solesmes; for reasons of diplomacy, public approval of this arrangement by the English Congregation was necessary; but the precise nature of the agreements eluded him. A letter from Cardinal Vaughan soon cleared up the mystery. On 24 December

Farnborough abbey

1900, Vaughan sent Gasquet a packet of documents. The Cardinal explained in a covering letter that he was forwarding 'a formal and official letter on the Cathedral as agreed, together with the original and translation of the Abbot of Solesmes' letter.'[13] Cardinal Vaughan asked Gasquet to return Delatte's letters, but for the time being to 'use them with due reserve and discretion.' He pleaded with the Abbot to try and convince his fellow Benedictines 'that the course contemplated is the only practical one.' 'A generous approval of the English Benedictines,' Cardinal Vaughan concluded, 'would produce, I think, a most favourable impression upon the Church in England as showing a breadth and large mindedness, not always found in Ecclesiastics or in corporations.'[14] Vaughan did not comprehend the intricacies of ecclesiastical politics, and failed to understand the competition and rivalry between religious congregations of the same church. 'He was not a scholar, nor indeed an intellectual; as a member of one of the old Catholic families, he was brought up to accept without questioning the teaching and policy of the Church.'[15]

Cardinal Vaughan's 'formal and official letter' to the General Chapter of the English Benedictine Congregation traced the history of the construction of Westminster Cathedral, his desire to make the Divine Office an essential part of its life, and emphasized that he had naturally turned to the English Congregation first. The long connection of Benedictine monks with the memory and name of Westminster, and his personal and affectionate dealings with Downside since the 1840s, motivated this decision. Consequently, the Cardinal confessed that he owed 'an explanation of the position in which I now find myself.'[16] He pointed out that difficulties, which 'seemed almost insurmountable,' immediately jeopardized his plan for a monastic foundation at

Westminster Cathedral. He reduced the problem to one essential:

> viz. the difficulty of so adjusting the rights, the life and the action of two independent Bodies – such as a Body of Regulars who by their Constitution are also Missioners, and a body of Secular Missionary Priests within the same Cathedral – as to preserve intact the rights of each and yet maintain that perfect peace and harmony which is the first condition in a work of co-operation.[17]

Westminster, being the metropolitan cathedral and the centre of the English hierarchy, care of the parish and the public devotions in the church should properly be under the control of the secular clergy. Consequently, this 'would at once confine the action of any religious Body attached to the Cathedral to the daily choral rendering of the Liturgy.'

The Cardinal's logic led to the following conclusion: the character of the English Benedictine Congregation necessarily excluded it from performing the Divine Office. Although three years earlier Vaughan was ecstatic about the possibility of Downside Benedictines occupying the stalls of Westminster, he now illustrated for Gasquet one hindrance: '. . . it has been pointed out to me, and I admit with undeniable reason, that I could not expect a Religious Congregation like yours to sacrifice the missionary character of their Constitution by confining its members to the choral service of the Cathedral to its exclusion from all active work in the ministry.' Vaughan for some reason chose to ignore the recent changes in the English Benedictine Constitution, which downplayed the missionary and emphasized the monastic character of the Order. He also argued that two separate and independent bodies of religious men, with their respective superiors and entrusted with similar tasks in the same church, 'would involve too great a risk for either of us to consider it prudent or wise to make the attempt.'[18]

Yet Cardinal Vaughan saw no problems or incongruities in approaching the French monks. The absence of a missionary or active apostolic life attracted him to the Solesmes Congregation: '. . . their Constitutions confine their vocation to the solemn rendering of the Office, and forbid them to take part in the work of the ministry and other external work, such as the foundation of Colleges etc. . . .' 'Here,' the Cardinal put to Gasquet, 'seems to be a solution of the difficulty that has arisen.' Points of possible friction and conflict would also be reduced to a minimum if the French, rather than English monks, conducted the worship in Westminster Cathedral. The contemplative and academic character of the Solesmes Congregation would not clash with pastoral duties, which would be the prerogative of the secular clergy. Vaughan admitted that nothing definite had been decided. Out of courtesy, he approached the English monks, '. . . the Body with which I have already been in communication,' to inform them of his present plan. The Abbot of Solesmes, he confessed, was eager to settle in London. Consequently, 'I have received from him a reply full of generous sentiments, and of respect for his Anglo-Benedictine Brethren, with the sketch of a plan that is perfectly satisfactory to myself as a basis for a tentative agreement.'[19] Vaughan had also enclosed Delatte's letter of June 1899 which spelled out the latter's proposals.

But the transfer of liturgical duties to these monks was not all Vaughan envisioned. The Solesmes settlement 'would in due time become independent and not continue as a dependency on the Mother House abroad.'

Solesmes abbey

This suggestion must have shocked and disturbed Abbot Gasquet. Not only was he asked to relinquish the honour of chanting the Latin office in Westminster Cathedral to a group of French monks, but he was also requested to give his approval to the existence of a permanent French monastery attached to the Cathedral. The Cardinal ended his letter in a manner which appeared insensitive, and even insulting, to the proud English Congregation:

> I am, therefore, anxious to lay this matter before you as Abbot President of the English Benedictines, and to act in such manner with you as should render it impossible for anyone to feel that an affront has been offered to the Anglo-Benedictine Congregation, or that they have been treated by me without consideration and courtesy. I have, therefore, ventured to send you this letter, and to say that, if you see any other practical arrangement that would be more satisfactory to you, I shall be pleased to examine it with you.[20]

Cardinal Vaughan had seriously underestimated the pride of the English Benedictine Congregation. Like Wiseman fifty years earlier, he miscalculated the homage, reverence, and tradition attached to the memory of Westminster. It must be served by English monks; to invite a foreign order would be virtually sacrilegious. Vaughan simply misread the sensitivity of the English Benedictines. 'What had seemed to the Cardinal just an act of fellowship between men working for a common cause, to the English Benedictines presented itself, and not unnaturally, in a very different light . . . they thought it an impossible proposal . . .'[21]

Before the opening of the Chapter of the English Benedictine Congregation, scheduled for February, Abbot Gasquet had determined that Vaughan's proposal, idealistic but unworkable, must be defeated. He began to formulate his opposition which would be presented to the Chapter. He believed that the Cardinal's dream to build a new Westminster was foolish. The Abbey of Westminster was dead, and to attempt a resurrection, 'ridiculous.'[22] Before considering co-operation with the foreign monks, Gasquet had to demand from the Cardinal a detailed schedule of duties the English would perform. 'What then is the work,' he queried, 'the members of the venerable Eng[lish] Cong[regation] are ... to take part in?' He maintained that it was 'difficult to believe that such a scheme should be calmly put forth by the Sol[esmes] O.S.B.'[23] 'Still more difficult,' he explained,

> to conceive a state of mind which would permit them to believe that we – members of a body which has come down ... unbroken ... from the days of St Augustine ... should not only calmly permit without protest such a scheme to be initiated, but were to be invited to assist in our own public degradation.[24]

Consequently, the Abbot President of the English Congregation determined to defeat Cardinal Vaughan's plan to bring the French monks into central London. If the English Benedictines refused to assist the French, or if the English conveyed a feeling of outrage or embarrassment, then this silly idea would certainly fail.

Despite Cardinal Vaughan's negotiation with the French and his communications with Abbot Gasquet, some of his public statements and actions demonstrated his indecision. A homily he preached at the Downside foundation at Ealing, for example, gave the impression that he still hoped that the Ealing monks would help at Westminster Cathedral. In his remarks, Vaughan thanked the Benedictine Fathers and rejoiced in the fact that 'the great and ancient Order of St Benedict should have full representation in the Diocese of Westminster.'[25] Vaughan expressed the gratitude of his archdiocese at the success of the monks, and urged the parishioners to support their new monastic foundation. *The Tablet*, in conclusion, drew attention to the role of the Benedictines in London: 'in no unseemly haste they have satisfied the wants of the day, but they have laid their lines for the future... [the new Ealing Church] is intended to serve for monastic, collegiate, and parochial purposes.'[26] While conversation progressed in England, the French Congregation was puzzled at the silence and the inaction of Cardinal Vaughan in failing to issue the formal invitation to come to Britain.

Abbot Delatte continued to be positive about a Solesmes foundation in London, and he related this optimism to his friend, Bishop Gilbert. The Bishop's response was typical of his earlier letters: 'I rejoice deeply with you at the vitality and expansion of this dear family.'[27] The delay on the part of Cardinal Vaughan constituted another matter, and the Bishop believed an explanation could be found in the area of international affairs:

> As to Westminster, I had seen, since the beginning of the Transvaal Affair, that if this noble creation would not become impossible, it would be temporarily or indefinitely postponed. One can see that there is a ferocious wave of 'Gallophobia,' and there may, or rather there must, arise from this incident, international strife, despite our cowardly action, strife which delays, very obviously, the taking possession [which is] so much the target of a French monastic element.[28]

Fr Ferdinand Cabrol

Westminster Cathedral does not appear in the correspondence of the French officials until October 1900, and here Abbot Delatte finally expressed his frustration over the delay on the part of Cardinal Vaughan.

Delatte's uneasiness about Vaughan's hesitation became clear early in this letter. 'It is true that I accepted Westminster in principle, but nevertheless under conditions which, after a year and a half, have not yet been formally accepted, since no notification has come to me.'[29] As in the case of Bishop Gilbert, Delatte recognized the importance of nationalism and foreign affairs in the negotiations. Delatte informed Cabrol that the Cardinal's 'caprices over the Boer War and over the Dreyfus Case were deeply displeasing to me ... It does not attract me very much to enter into very close relations with a man who is capable of swerving to that extent.' But Delatte understood the reason for this attitude: 'He will have his Englishman's soul forever, until the hour when he renders it to God.' The important section of the letter, however, contained the Abbot's decision to modify seriously his earlier arrangements with Cardinal Vaughan. One reason for a reconsideration was the rumour that Gasquet would be the next Archbishop of Westminster: '. . . what will our position be? Will we even have time to establish ourselves?' But the crucial reason which forced Delatte to back out was Cardinal Vaughan's lack of direction.

Abbot Delatte told Cabrol of Farnborough that at the present he could only contribute a reduced contingent of Solesmes monks to the proposed London foundation. 'The effort which I could have agreed to last year in order to form with you the Westminster community, I could no longer undertake today with a reduced house.' He related that he felt '. . . free as far as England was concerned' and had already sent monks to another foundation, St Paul's, Wisques,[30] and had promised to send more. So the Abbot then asked Cabrol if the Farnborough community might be willing to transfer to Westminster: 'Would you be numerous enough with the few men the English congregation might furnish you with? It is up to you to see.' The Abbot concluded that he was 'forced to dissociate' himself for one reason: '. . . the Cardinal can blame no one but himself; his silence of a year seemed to me to be equivalent to an abandonment.'[31] Bishop Gilbert offered some predictable advice. He realized that any immediate solution was out of the question, but cautioned against Delatte's abrupt change of policy: 'I am more disheartened and overwhelmed by the present ignominy than I am dumbfounded and discouraged by the announcement of a decisive ruinous solution which to me is *impossible*.'[32] In the next month, Gilbert again begged Delatte to reconsider: 'in such a far-reaching undertaking a few years spent in preambles and in cautiously feeling one's way along are not much, when one thinks of this seizure of the lofty orthodox and doctrinal apostolate of England, which is what I perceive under all this music you are asked for.'[33] As Bishop Gilbert was warning Delatte against any rash action, the General Chapter of the English Congregation met at Downside Abbey.

6. THE ABBOT VERSUS THE ARCHBISHOP

The General Chapter of the English Congregation convened at Downside Abbey in February 1901. Speculation and mystery surround the debates and discussions concerning Westminster Cathedral, but it appears that Gasquet's violent opposition to Cardinal Vaughan's Solesmes proposal captured the consensus of the membership, which probably had serious reservations itself about the plan. Written on behalf of the Congregation on 13 February, Gasquet's report thanked Cardinal Vaughan for the 'kind communication of December 24th . . . [but] the authorities of our Congregation have as yet never received from you any definite offer to serve your Cathedral.'[1] According to Gasquet, the Chapter noted the anxiety of the Cardinal not to insult or affront the English Benedictines. Moreover, the Abbot President stated that the Chapter had never rejected or abandoned its traditional claim to Westminster, which Vaughan had suggested in the past. 'We would willingly entertain and consider any scheme for our serving . . . Westminster,' Gasquet reported, 'which your Eminence, conjointly with your Canons, would formulate, provided it was not inconsistent with the vocation of the English Benedictines as recently determined by the Holy See.'

Castigating the Cardinal Archbishop for his failure to make a firm and detailed commitment to the English monks, even after promising the native congregation the honour of serving at the new Westminster Cathedral, Abbot Gasquet informed Vaughan of the mind of the Chapter. The English Benedictines 'cannot be expected to give either assistance or countenance to the establishment of any community of foreign Benedictines in our English Metropolitan Cathedral.'[2] This action alone demolished the original agreement between Vaughan and Abbot Delatte. Moreover, hurt pride and a broken promise contributed to the Chapter's hostile mood: 'Such a foundation cannot fail to be regarded as a serious reflection on our venerable Congregation, more especially in view of your Eminence's public declarations that you intended to establish English Benedictines at Westminster.' As far as the Chapter was concerned it would not condone any French presence in London. If monks were to be at Westminster, they must be English. The blame must rest with the Cardinal if no Benedictines graced the choir of his cathedral. 'The Abbot-President and his Assistants,' he reminded Vaughan, are ready at any time to consider any scheme which may be proposed by Your Eminence and your Chapter.'[3]

Along with this official notification of the General Chapter's decision, Abbot Gasquet enclosed his personal criticism of Cardinal Vaughan's scheme. 'You asked me to be quite frank,' he wrote in a letter of introduction, and 'I hope that you will not think that I am outspoken in criticizing the French scheme.'[4] He told Vaughan that he could not believe that the Cardinal had 'really studied the French Abbot's letter, for the proposals made are so very different to any that you told me you had received from Solesmes.' As an introduction to his long, detailed and fatal critique of the so-called French scheme, the Abbot pinpointed the chief motive for his opposition to Vaughan's plan: 'at any rate you will see from my criticism that we could not, consistently with our oaths to maintain our rights

Prior Edmund Ford

and privileges, do anything but oppose the proposal of the Solesmes Fathers to come over here to set up a rival Congregation.'

Abbot Gasquet's lengthy diatribe demonstrated his scholarship, his knowledge of English religious history, and his fierce determination to prevent the French monks from establishing themselves at Westminster Cathedral. Gasquet sketched the history of the negotiations between the Cardinal and the English Congregation concerning the possibility of the latter staffing the London Cathedral. Gasquet reminded him that the initiative came from the Cardinal: 'You asked me to be the intermediary between yourself and the Superiors of the English Benedictine congregation to obtain a body of monks for the purpose.' 'Your Eminence came to us; and I am confident that we should never of ourselves have thought of what you proposed.' Gasquet admitted that he had realized the difficulties involved, the jealousies the plan would stir us, and how 'it would hamper us in any future undertakings.' 'And only on the supposition that we were serving the broader interests of the Church in England could we have been justified,' Gasquet stated, 'would the Benedictines of Downside have ever abandoned some of their present commitments'.'

Gasquet reminded Vaughan that he told him immediately 'that the only way in which a scheme such as yours could possibly work would be to entrust the entire management of the Cathedral to the body of monks.' Due care had also to be taken to preserve the position and rights of the Cathedral Chapter. Abbot Gasquet continued to point the accusing finger. It was Vaughan who suggested that the monks take over two missions which would ultimately be incorporated into the Cathedral parish 'in order that we might get to know the district in which we have to work. . . .' It was Vaughan who publicly announced on many occasions that he had requested the English Benedictines to take up this work. 'If then there has been any error as to what your Eminence wanted of us,' Abbot Gasquet reasoned, 'the mistake did not originate with us.'

Abbot Gasquet accused the Cardinal of deception in negotiating with the Solesmes monks. He acknowledged that he had heard rumours that the Cardinal was 'in treaty with foreigners who had agreed to come merely to act as a paid choir to sing the offices.'[6] But he maintained that he 'treated the matter as merely one of the many unfounded stories constantly being spread about one in your exalted position.' Another reason why the Abbot dismissed these stories as unfounded gossip was Cardinal Vaughan's public and private statements of support for the English Congregation, and his desire to have at Westminster Cathedral 'the one body which had come down in unbroken succession from the days of St Augustine. . . . ' His accusation of ecclesiastical duplicity emphasized the illogical point in Vaughan's plan: 'You now, however, ask me not only to put before our Fathers a scheme proposed by the Abbot of Solesmes for serving your Cathedral, but to induce them to facilitate its working by giving their approval to the French fathers coming to London and even by actively co-operating in *their* work at your Cathedral.'

Patriotism and national pride played its part in the bruised feelings of the English Benedictines:

It would of course be useless to disguise the fact that we English Benedictines, who have been connected with this country for so many centuries and who have borne the burden and heat of the day during the years of persecution, cannot

see with pleasure a position, which must be
regarded as the most prominent occupied by
the Order in England, assigned to foreigners.[7]

He admitted that he did not expect Vaughan to
appreciate the *convenances de choses* between different
congregations of Benedictine monks, but he could not
'comprehend how ordinary feelings of delicacy did not
force the French fathers to at once decline your offer to
intrude themselves into the province of another well
established congregation in another country.' Vaughan
might have been naive, but according to Gasquet the
Solesmes Congregation had broken ecclesiastical proto-
col. Had he been asked to establish an English abbey on
French soil, Gasquet told the Cardinal that 'we should
never dream of setting up a rival to a Benedictine
congregation already existing in France.'[8] The English
Abbot attacked the French for even considering the
Cardinal's proposals, but finally excused Vaughan
because he 'could not be expected to understand this
and not unnaturally desired to secure what appeared to
suit your purpose best.'

The Cardinal must shoulder the blame for a large
part of the *débâcle*. Gasquet noted that the original
letter from Abbot Delatte differed in essential points
from the English translation, which had been sent to
Downside Abbey from Archbishop's House. Gasquet
also called attention to his meeting at Mill Hill with
Cardinal Vaughan. Here, according to Abbot Gasquet,
the Cardinal stated that the French 'were willing to
come to Westminster to do nothing beyond the singing
of the office, to take no part in the management of the
Cathedral and not to look for any influence of work
beyond the monastery walls.'[9] Delatte's letter suggested

Dom Aidan Gasquet

more than this. Gasquet, therefore, listed the aspects which proved that the French had more in mind than the singing of the Divine Office: they refused to be bound by any written agreement; they wanted a monastery built for them in Ashley Gardens (adjacent to the Cathedral); and Abbot Delatte had even admitted that the monks he would send to London possessed either weak or horrible voices! Abbot Gasquet argued that the Solesmes monks could not contribute much to the liturgy, pointing out that Delatte admitted that 'hired and trained singers, the choir school and choir master. . .'[10] must assume the duty for the Cathedral's worship. Why, then, did the Solesmes monks want to settle in London?

> It will be seen by the above that the French Fathers contemplate very much more than the mere singing of their office and practically require to have the management of the Cathedral with the small exception of matters strictly parochial, all of which are moreover to be confined to a side chapel . . . They have visions of people resorting to them for advice and direction . . . they still hope to find in the neighbourhood of your Cathedral a well kept hotel 'where priests, religious and others' who could not be accommodated within the monastery, might lodge.[11]

The Abbot of Solesmes, he believed, desired nothing less than the establishment of a colony of French monks in London. Gasquet even accused Abbot Delatte of ingratitude. 'It is difficult to believe', the Abbot told Vaughan, 'that it could have been put forth seriously by Benedictine brethren who have received nothing but kindness from us and who owe their very presence at Farnborough to my own suggestion to the late

Bishop of Portsmouth.'[12] Frenchmen cannot comprehend the English Catholic mind, and their presence at Westminster would insult the pride of the English monks and the nation. Therefore, Abbot Gasquet concluded, it would be impossible that the 'Monks of a congregation already existing in England should calmly permit without protest the initiation of such an infringement of our rights and privileges, but accept their invitation to co-operate in their scheme and thus assist in the dismemberment of our own body and in our own public degradation.'[13] Gasquet closed this long letter by excusing the Cardinal from any malicious intent: 'it is obvious to every one of us that you could not have understood the proposals made in the Abbot of Solesmes letter.'[14]

The refusal of the English Benedictine monks to co-operate with the French, and their strong protests over the wisdom and prudence of Cardinal Vaughan's proposal, effectively destroyed the Cardinal's hope to have Benedictines associated with Westminster Cathedral. Yet, according to Snead-Cox, 'those who were much with Cardinal Vaughan in those days knew that he received the reply of the English Benedictines without disappointment.'[15] Vaughan still believed that the French were straightforward and honest, even generous, in their dealings with him. Vaughan replied to Abbot Gasquet's critique and tried to assure him that the French monks had not attacked or maligned their English counterparts: 'I should assure you that they have spoken and acted with great kindness and consideration for the English Benedictine Congregation.'[16]

Cardinal Vaughan refused to accept Gasquet's 'interpretation of the Abbot's [Delatte's] designs,' and explained how the Solesmes Abbot desired to act in a 'friendly way and in co-operation with them.' The Cardinal apologized for the shoddy translation of

Delatte's letter, informing Gasquet that some of his objections to the content of the letter were meaningless since these had already been renegotiated.

Gasquet's reply to Cardinal Vaughan's attempted apology and explanation of his Solesmes plan revealed that the English Abbot would still not yield in his criticisms. Four points were clear and obvious: In the first place, Gasquet still maintained that the 'Abbot of Solesmes's meaning seemed perfect [sic] clear and definite.'[17] No amount of rationalization could erase the fact that the French Benedictines intended to establish a permanent monastic foundation on English soil. Gasquet then singled out the main problem which troubled the negotiations of the past five years: the 'whole matter of West[minster] involved. . .great diff[iculties].' The history and heritage attached to the name of Westminster recalled the greatness of Britain's past; a French association with this hallowed tradition would produce vindictiveness and hatred on the part of the English. His third point addressed the question of rivalry. Gasquet claimed that there existed a 'strong feeling . . . among secular priests against religious,' and consequently if any Benedictine, native or foreign, were to conduct the liturgy at Westminster Cathedral, conflict and bitterness would explode within English Catholicism. In light of this observation, Abbot Gasquet's fourth point offered a solution, which the Cardinal eventually adopted. To put an end to the tension between the French and English Benedictines, and also to eliminate any animosity between the religious and secular clergy of England, he suggested that secular priests perform the ceremonies. In addition to this, a choral school might be established to supply the

Downside abbey

trained singers to perform vespers and the High Mass. Gasquet's proposals were welcome news to Vaughan, who saw a quiet way out of the Westminster Cathedral problem. Until the spring of 1901, the Cardinal had no idea of the difficulties arising from the questions of jurisdiction, problems of nationality, and the reverence for the memory of Westminster. Vaughan's biographer recorded that 'he learned of the breaking off of his negotiations with the French and English monks with equanimity, but perhaps a truer word would be "relief".'[18]

Since the English Benedictines refused to sanction his plan, Cardinal Vaughan informed the French monks that it would be impossible for them to come to London. He still had no idea that the French had already changed their minds. Vaughan, therefore, wrote to Fr Cabrol, their superior, telling him the news that the English monks had refused to co-operate with the French. Cabrol replied relating that he had been keen on forming a 'schola at Westminster capable of singing Gregorian Chant . . . .'[19] Saddened but not shocked by the actions of the English Benedictines, he informed Vaughan that he possessed little knowledge of 'the details of the decision taken by the General Chapter of which Your Eminence writes.' He admitted that he was 'not surprised because . . . [he] knew of the very determined opposition of the English Benedictines to the project of Your Eminence.' The Cardinal eventually informed Abbot Delatte of the altered situation, and sent him a copy of Gasquet's letter which announced the decision of the General Chapter of the English Benedictines.

Cardinal Vaughan, however, still needed clerics to take charge of the services at Westminster. Even at this point, Cardinal Vaughan hoped that the English Benedictines might help. 'We are now in this impasse,' he told Gasquet, 'I said I am willing to consider a proposal from you: and you reply that you are willing to consider one from me.' It was no secret that the Cathedral Chapter had expressed serious reservations about Benedictine monks of any nationality working in the new cathedral. Gasquet's solution to the impasse was acceptable: why not relinquish to this body the duties which were previously to be entrusted to monks? Vaughan determined, therefore, 'to fall back upon a simpler and bolder solution and, to the huge delight of the whole archdiocese, decided to entrust the rendering of the liturgy of the Cathedral to the Secular clergy.'[20] The Bishop-Auxiliary of the Archdiocese of Westminster, Bishop Brindle, conveyed Cardinal Vaughan's decision to a receptive Chapter.[21] At the 23 April meeting of 1901 Brindle announced that Vaughan 'had given up his intention of establishing Benedictine monks in the Westminster Cathedral for the singing of Divine Office.'[22]

Part of the failure to procure Benedictines for the new Westminster Cathedral could be traced to the words and deeds of the monks of Downside. 'The Benedictine monks in England had expressed their inability to undertake the task,' the Provost, Mgr Michael Barry, stated, 'and had declared their resolve of protesting before the Holy See, if Benedictine monks were introduced for the purpose mentioned from France.' Consequently, secular priests of Westminster Archdiocese, 'whose selection would be determined by their fitness for the work,' would now supervise and perform the liturgical services at the Westminster.

Cardinal Vaughan personally revealed this new plan for his clergy during the annual meeting of the Westminster Diocesan Synod in 1901. The Cardinal explained that an essential function of the new cathedral would be the performance of the Divine Office and celebration of High Mass. 'A high standard of church music and religious ceremonial must accompany the liturgy,' he told the priests, and 'its religious services should leave nothing to be desired as to solemnity and devotion.'[23] Vaughan concluded that originally he 'had thought of the great Benedictine Order, and had both publicly and privately expressed the hope that the Liturgical services of the Cathedral might be confided to their care.' However, 'difficulties had arisen that appeared insuperable.' The Cardinal assumed, therefore, that the secular clergy would gladly undertake this task, and he informed the Synod that the plans were already being considered by the Chapter. He declared that he saw many advantages in this, and 'one thing only was more important, and that was the establishment in the Cathedral of a really high standard of Liturgical service, both as to music and ceremonial.' The Archbishop ended his report by expressing his confidence in the ability of the clergy to undertake this new and important charge. But he also issued a warning to the Synod: 'If they failed, it would become necessary to call in some body of men who make the Liturgy their one and only work.' This threat demonstrated that Benedictine monks might still be recruited if needed.

The Roman Catholic press had prepared the public for this change. A few years earlier, *The Tablet* had reported Cardinal Vaughan's earnest wish to bring Benedictine monks into the precincts of his new cathedral. Its columns now announced that the monks would not be invited; the honour of conducting the cathedral's liturgy would be the work of the secular clergy instead. The article stated that 'much public interest has for some time past centered on the question

An aerial view of Ealing

how and by whom the solemn Liturgical Offices of the Church are to be rendered in the new Cathedral.'[24] *The Tablet* noted the 'unforseen difficulties which had arisen when it had been proposed to call in the services of a Religious Order for the daily religious chant of the Liturgy. . . .' Consequently, 'the Cardinal Archbishop announced that he gladly availed himself of the readiness of the Secular clergy to take up the work.' The clergy, the report stated, were overjoyed and eager. Nonetheless, a touch of nostalgia and sadness crept into the columns of *The Tablet*: 'We confess we would have been glad to see the cowls of the Benedictines back in Westminster.'

Some historical link or bond existed between the two Westminsters, and it might have been fitting for monks to be associated with the new cathedral. But 'apart from the old associations which cluster around the site of Westminster, is it not after all better, and more in accordance with the fitness of things, that the Secular clergy should themselves render the Liturgy in the new Cathedral?'[25] Moreover, it would have been anomalous to entrust the services of the cathedral, which represented all England, to a single religious order, the Benedictines. For this purpose, Vaughan 'obtained permission from Rome to increase the number of Canons of the Metropolitan Chapter from twelve to eighteen, and make provisions for a body of eighteen Cathedral Chaplains.'[26]

In the spring of 1901, the Chapter of Westminster Cathedral 'uniformly declared its entire concurrence with the proposal made by his Eminence with respect to the Choir Service of the Cathedral.'[27] And in May 1902, the Divine Office was sung for the first time in Westminster Cathedral. Cardinal Vaughan, therefore, achieved the singing of plain chant, the loyalty and gratitude of the Cathedral Chapter and peace between religious and secular clergy, but not the services of Benedictine monks – French or English.

The failure of Cardinal Vaughan to grace his new and magnificent cathedral with the melodies of the Benedictines chanting the Divine Office demonstrated that English Catholicism was not as unified as some tend to believe. The Catholic press of the period constantly ridiculed the divisions, squabbles, and conflicts within the Established Church, and painted Roman Catholicism as the one, unified, catholic church. According to this argument, the division of High and Low Church did not plague Roman Catholicism; evangelical and Anglo-Catholic parties, some boasted, did not trouble the Catholic community. The conflict concerning the performance of the liturgical duties at Westminster Cathedral, however, revealed that jealousy and rivalry also beset the Roman Catholics.

Within English Catholicism, competition between the religious and secular clergy could be traced back to the Middle Ages. Cardinal Vaughan's initial impulse to entrust the liturgy at Westminster to the English Benedictines fanned and renewed the fires of distrust. Although not as violent as in the past, the secular clergy resented Vaughan's proposal and successfully resisted his desire to hand over Westminster Cathedral to the monks of Downside Abbey. The monks at Ealing were aware of this tension and animosity. One of them, Dom Gilbert Dolan OSB, wrote to Downside and noted 'a certain antagonism to us lately in the curia at Archbishop's House . . . as though the anti-French manifesto with regard to the serving the new Cathedral must be visited on our heads.'[28] Dolan concluded succinctly, '*that* scheme I hear is "off", and we must suffer for the rebuff its proposer has received from the Chapter of Westminster.'

Sadly, there was not unity of purpose within the Benedictine Order itself; altruism and service to the Church were sacrificed to national pride, patriotism, and inter-congregational feuds. If the services of the French monks were to be obtained instead of the English monks, two conditions were necessary: the English Benedictines must give their public approval; and the same congregation must supply some monks to assist the French, who would receive the honour and glory. Abbot Aidan Gasquet vigorously opposed both, and thus he ensured that the French monks, who already had had second thoughts, would reject Vaughan's invitation. If Westminster was not in English Benedictine hands, French Benedictines would certainly not occupy its stalls.

The troubles over Westminster Cathedral also revealed some insights into the personality of Cardinal Vaughan, the spokesman of English Roman Catholicism. By nature a romantic, he planned the construction of his new cathedral complete with a contingent of Benedictines. For the Cardinal and some pious Catholics, it would become a new Westminster arising from the destruction of the Reformation. Vaughan eventually emerged from the problems he created successfully, but one can see his ecclesiastical naivety and unreasonable idealism in that he actually believed that the secular clergy would relinquish their claim to officiate in the new cathedral to the Benedictine monks. Gasquet believed that Cardinal Vaughan showed his true colours in the problems he created with regard to the Benedictines and Westminster Cathedral. According to him, 'it is very sad how completely out of all touch he appears to be with everyone.'[29] But there were wider implications:

Ealing abbey and school

'Altogether the general outlook in England is very depressing and one has to say one's prayers and mind one's own business as best one may.' More importantly, 'the position of Catholics made by Cardinal Manning has been very much lowered.'

The Cardinal conceived the Roman Church to be a universal organization which transcended national boundaries. He quickly discovered, however, that nationalism was not confined to politics and foreign policy; it also infected religious groups. The fierce and dogged opposition of the English monks to the French shattered Vaughan's illusion. In the end, the secular clergy won the privilege to conduct the services at Westminster, and the troubles quickly faded away. In 1947, Dom Bruno Hicks OSB, the former Abbot of Downside, correctly commented on Cardinal Vaughan's solution to the Westminster controversy:

> Whatever sentimental regret may be felt on historical grounds that the Benedictine monks are not again at Westminster, no one can deny that the Divine Office and the Liturgical services are carried out in the Cathedral to-day in a manner comparable to that which obtained in the great abbeys of England before the Reformation.[30]

7. CATHEDRAL RESPLENDENT: THE FRUITION
OF A DREAM

Thus the year 1902 marked the opening of Westminster Cathedral. 'You will be pleased to hear,' Cardinal Vaughan wrote to his friend Lady Herbert of Lea, 'that we had the whole of the Divine Office and High Mass for the first time on Ascension Day, in the Chapter Hall.'[1] He could not disguise his pride: 'the Hall has been arranged like the Sistine Chapel and looks beautiful.' Worship and liturgy continued to occupy an important part in the Cardinal's plans for his new cathedral. In addition to entrusting the liturgy to his secular clergy, Vaughan founded a choir school, and the spirit of Benedictinism lingered here: the first director of music and choir master, R R Terry, came from Downside School. Soon afterwards Cardinal Vaughan formed a College of Cathedral Chaplains.

During that same year, J F Bentley, architect of the cathedral, died. The Cardinal paid tribute to him and remarked that 'he put the whole of his life and soul into the Cathedral and it killed him, not the designing but the carrying it out.'[2] It was fitting that on 26 June 1903 Cardinal Vaughan's own requiem was the first large religious service to be conducted in the cathedral he laboured to construct. Vaughan's successors at Westminster – Francis Bourne (1861-1935), Arthur Hinsley (1865-1943), Bernard Griffin (1899-1956), William Godfrey (1889-1963), John Heenan (1905-1975), and Basil Hume (1923-) – all continued to enrich the cathedral, making it a proud symbol of Roman Catholicism and a fitting place of worship.

The connection between London and the Benedictine monks which Cardinal Vaughan had originally proposed also became a reality. The Downside mission in Ealing prospered. The parish grew rapidly, and the church had to be enlarged during the century to meet the increase in parishioners. In 1902, Dom Sebastian Cave OSB, opened a school in Ealing to educate young boys with traditional Benedictine ideals. The current enrolment is approximately eight hundred. Alongside parish and school, the monastic community quickly showed signs of permanence. In 1916 Ealing became a priory, but still remained dependent on Downside. It was recognized as an independent priory in 1947, and was raised to the rank of abbey in 1955. In addition to parochial and educational responsibilities, Ealing Abbey also sponsors prayer and retreat centres.

The fortunes of the French Benedictines did not fare as well; the Solesmes monks did come to England, but under difficult circumstances. In 1901, the French government's anti-clerical policies forced them to flee France and journey to England, where they took refuge on the Isle of Wight. It was not until 1922 that these Benedictines returned to Solesmes. The French foundation at Farnborough grew steadily. In 1903, it was created an abbey, and Dom Ferdinand Cabrol was elected its first Abbot, an office he held until his death in 1937. The monastery is currently affiliated with the Subiaco Congregation. In addition to teaching and pastoral duties, the abbey also operates a press.

The relationship between Westminster Cathedral and the Benedictines became more intimate in 1976 when Abbot Basil Hume OSB, of Ampleforth, was appointed Archbishop of Westminster by Pope Paul VI. An ecumenical service and Latin vespers at nearby Westminster Abbey concluded the celebrations surrounding his installation on 25 March 1976. The

The Archbishop's cathedra

Catholic press quickly pointed out the symbolism of this ceremony: 'the visit is at the invitation of the Dean of Westminster and will be the first time for more than 400 years that this service has been sung in the Abbey in the traditional Latin plainsong.'³ *The Universe* noted that Latin vespers had a double significance for the new Archbishop of Westminster. In the first place, it emphasized the importance Hume placed on prayer and, secondly, it demonstrated 'his conviction that Christian unity is best achieved by "praying churches".' The article ended happily with a reference to the 'Benedictine heritage of the new Archbishop.'

To commemorate the 1500th anniversary of St Benedict's birth, a special mass was celebrated in Westminster Cathedral in July 1980. The cathedral choir and Benedictines from England and abroad provided the music: 'Trumpets and tympani greeted a procession of 300 monks as they entered Westminster Cathedral last Friday', *The Universe* reported.⁴ 'With 130 Benedictines nuns they represented the 44 monasteries and priories of Benedictines and Cistercians . . . in England.' After this service, the monks and nuns walked to Westminster Abbey to sing Latin Vespers. The press did not fail to grasp the significance of this. 'The history behind the Abbey setting, the united prayer, the presence of the Anglican Benedictines, opened vistas of a long-term ecumenism rooted in the pursuit of a spiritual ideal tested by time.' During that summer of 1980, therefore, Cardinal Vaughan's dream to unite Benedictinism with the hallowed name of Westminster was finally realized.

ENDNOTES

Introduction

1. O. Chadwick, *The Victorian Church*, Part I (London: Adam and Charles Black, 1972), p.271. For a description of Roman Catholics in England in the nineteenth century and their growing self-awareness and intense pride, see H. Jedin, ed., *History of the Church: The Church in the Industrial Age*, vol. 9 (London: Burns and Oates, 1981), pp.135-144.

2. O. Chadwick, op. cit., p.290.

3. Ibid., p.291.

1. Catholicism in England from the Reformation

1. O. Chadwick, *The Reformation* (Middlesex: Penguin Books, 1972), p.31.

2. Ibid., p.33.

3. Ibid., p.39.

4. Ibid., p.109.

5. M. Powicke, *The Reformation in England* (London: Oxford University Press, 1973), p.28.

6. O. Chadwick, ibid. p.105.

7. G. Cragg, *The Church and the Age of Reason 1648-1789* (Middlesex: Penguin Books, 1972), p.139.

8. J. Bossy, *The English Catholic Community 1570-1850* (London: Darton, Longman, Todd, 1976), p.296.

9. Ibid., p.297.

10. O. Chadwick, *The Victorian Church*, Part I. p.278.

11. J. D. Holmes, *More Roman than Rome: English Catholicism in the Nineteenth Century* (London: Burns and Oates, 1978), p.74.

2. A Cathedral for Westminster

1. O. Chadwick, *The Victorian Church*, Part II (London: Adam and Charles Black, 1972), p.242.

2. E. S. Purcell, *Life of Cardinal Church Archbishop of Westminster* (London: MacMillan Co., 1896), p.353.

3. Quoted in S. L. Leslie, *Henry Edward Manning: His Life and Labour* (London: Burns and Oates, 1921), p.171.

4. Ibid., pp.171-172.

5. E. S. Purcell, ibid p.354.

6. S. Leslie, ibid. p.171.

7. A. McCormack, *Cardinal Vaughan* (London: Burns and Oates, 1966), p.289.

8. J. G. Snead-Cox, *The Life of Cardinal Vaughan* vol. 2 (London: Burns and Oates, 1910), p.317.

9. E. Norman, *The English Catholic Church in the Nineteenth Century* (Oxford: Clarendon Press, 1984), p.345.

10. Ibid.

11. J. D. Holmes, *More Roman than Rome: English Catholicism in the Nineteenth Century*, p.199.

12. E. Norman, *Roman Catholicism in England from the Elizabethan Settlement to the Second Vatican Council* (Oxford: Oxford University Press, 1985), p.95.

13. Ibid.

14. For biographies on Cardinal Vaughan see: A Mill Father, *Remembered In Blessing: The Courtfield Story* (London: Sands Co., 1969); and J. G. Snead-Cox, *The Life of Cardinal Vaughan* 2 vols. (London: Herbert and David, 1910).

15. J. D. Holmes, Ibid., p.201.

16. Ibid.

17. J. G. Snead-Cox, ibid vol. 2, pp.319-320.

18. A. McCormack, ibid. p.288.

19. Ibid. p.291.

20. *The Tablet* (London), 6 July 1895.

21. Ibid.

22. J. G. Snead-Cox, ibid., vol. 2, p.347.

23. Ibid.

24. Ibid., p.348.

25. For a history of the English Benedictines in the nineteenth century see British Museum, *The Benedictines in Britain* (London: The British Library, 1980); E. Cruise, "Development of the Religious Orders," in *The English Catholics 1850-1950* (London: Burns and Oates, 1950); and B. Green, *The English Benedictine Congregation* (London: Burns and Oates, 1950); and B. Greeen, *The English Benedictine Congregation* (London: Catholic Truth Society, 1980). The following biographies are also useful: B. Hicks, *Hugh Edmund Ford* (London: Sands Co., 1947); and S. Leslie, *Cardinal Gasquet: A Memoir* (New York: P. J. Kenedy, 1953).

26. B. Hicks, ibid.

27. Vaughan to Ford, 5 May 1896, Ford Papers, Ealing Abbey Archives, London.

28. Ford to Vaughan, 6 May 1896, Ford Papers.

29. B. Hicks, ibid., p.73.

30. B. Hicks, ibid., p.14.

31. Ford to Vaughan, 5 June 1896, Ford Papers.

32. Ibid.

33. Vaughan to Ford, 17 June 1896, Vaughan Papers, Archives of Westminster Archdiocese, Archbishop's House, London.

34. Ibid.

35. For a description of the governance of the English Benedictine Congregation, see Hicks, ibid., pp.100-137. Hicks also presents an excellent discussion of the changes forced upon the English Congregation by Rome during this period, the so-called 'Constitutional Crisis.' B. Green, *The English Benedictine Congregation*, pp.82-87, also has a good discussion.

36. Ford to Fathers, 18 August 1896, Ford Papers.

37. O'Gorman to Ford, 29 September 1896, Ford Papers.

38. Petition, 10 October 1896, Ealing Abbey Archives.

39. Vaughan to Ford, 28 October 1896, Ford Papers. The Ealing Archives has a copy of the Roman rescript.

40. J. G. Snead-Cox, ibid., vol. 2, p.347.

41. Ibid., pp.347-348.

42. *Minutes of the Cathedral Chapter of Westminster, 31 January 1878 to 7 November 1899*, vol. 4, 4 December 1894, St. Mary's Presbytery. East Finchley, London.

43. Ibid., 8 January 1895.

44. See pp.14f.

45. *Minutes of the Cathedral Chapter of Westminster, 31 January 1878 to 7 November 1899*, 6 October 1896.

46. Ibid., 3 November 1896.

47. J. G. Snead-Cox, ibid., vol. 2, pp.347-348.

48. Ford to Vaughan, 7 December 1898, Vaughan Papers, Archbishop's House.

49. Ibid.

50. Ibid.

51. Ibid.

52. Ibid.

53. J. G. Snead-Cox, ibid., vol. 2, p.349.

54. E. Cruise, *Development of the Religious Orders*, p.457. The author also notes that 'such Constitutions had been formed to allow the English Benedictines to concentrate all their energies upon missionary work at a time when the number of secular priests were woefully inadequate' p.457. See pp.30-31 for the radical changes imposed on the English Benedictine Constitutions by the Vatican. The British Library, *The Benedictines in Britain*, pp.97-99, presents a good discussion of the missionary character of the English Benedictines.

55. J. G. Snead-Cox, ibid., vol. 2, p.349. Prior Ford, however, was in favour of a more monastic as opposed to missionary spirit for the English monks. Yet he faced strong opposition from the General Chapter.

56. Ibid.

3. Saga of the French Monks

1. E. B. Koenker, *The Liturgical Renaissance in the Roman Catholic Church* (Chicago: University of Chicago Press, 1954), p.10.

2. Ibid.

3. J. A. Jungmann, *Public Worship* (London: Challoner Publication, 1957), p.30.

4. *New Catholic Encyclopedia*, s.v. 'Music of Solesmes.'

5. *The Tablet*, 1 June 1901.

6. The Ratisbon edition represented the liturgy and interpretation of a rival school.

7. 'Note of Dom Delatte,' Summer 1899, Delatte Papers, Solesmes Abbey Archives, France.

8. Ibid.

9. Bishop Abel Gilbert was the Bishop of Le Mans, the diocese in which the Abbey of Solesmes is situated, from 1894 to 1898. At the time of his correspondence with Delatte about the possibility of an English foundation, he was the titular Bishop of Arsinoe. He died in 1914.

10. Gilbert to Delatte, 10 June 1899, Delatte Papers.

11. Ibid.

12. Delatte to Vaughan, 11 June 1899, Vaughan Papers, Archbishop's House, p.1.

13. Ibid.

14. Ibid.

15. M. D. Knowles, *Cardinal Gasquet as an Historian* (London: The Athlone Press, 1957), p.3.

16. Ibid., pp.15-17.

17. Ibid., p.18.

18. Ibid., p.19.

19. Ibid.

20. See the following for the life of Cardinal Aidan Gasquet: D. Knowles, ibid., and S. Leslie, *Cardinal Gasquet: A Memoir* (New York: P. J. Kenedy, 1953).

21. Delatte to Vaughan, 11 June 1899, Vaughan Papers, Archbishop's House p.2.

22. Ibid.

23. Ibid.

24. Ibid., p.3.

25. Ibid., p.4.

26. Ibid., p.5.

27. In 1887 the Empress Eugenie established a monastery at Farnborough for Canons of the Premonstration Order. In 1895, monks from Solesmes replaced the Canons. There was also another French foundation on English soil. Because of anti-clericalism in France, monks from La Pierre-qui-vire established a foundation at Buckfast in 1882. It became independent in 1899 and an abbey in 1903.

28. Delatte to Vaughan, 11 June 1899, Vaughan Papers, Archbishop's House, p.6.

29. Ibid.

30. Ibid., p.7.

31. Ibid., p.8.

32. Ibid.

33. Moyes to Vaughan, 17 July 1899, Vaughan Papers, Archbishop's House. At the end of June, Cardinal Vaughan visited Abbot Delatte at Solesmes. There is no information available on the length or nature of the visit.

34. Ibid.

35. Moyes, 'Westminster Cathedral and the Monks of Solesmes: Memorandum,' July 1899, Vaughan Papers, Archbishop's House.

36. Ibid., p.2.

37. Ibid., p.3.

38. Ibid., p.4.

39. Ibid.

40. Ibid., p.6.

41. Ibid., p.7.

42. Ibid., p.8.

43. Moyes, 'The Westminster Cathedral and the Monks of Solesmes: Preliminary Articles of Agreement,' July 1899, Vaughan Papers, Archbishop's House.

44. Moyes to Vaughan, 17 July 1899, Vaughan Papers, Archbishop's House.

45. Ibid.

46. *The Tablet*, 18 February 1899.

47. Ibid.

48. Ibid.

49. Ibid.

50. *The Tablet*, 13 May 1899.

51. Ibid.

52. *The Tablet*, 1 July 1899; *The Times*, 30 June 1899; and *The Weekly Register*, 1 July 1899.

53. Ibid.

4. The Benedictines versus the Secular Clergy

1. *The Weekly Register*, 15 July 1899.

2. Ibid.

3. *The Catholic Times and Catholic Opinion* (London), 21 July 1899.

4. See pp.19f.

5. E. Cruise, *The Development of Religious Orders*, p.458.

6. B. Hicks, *Hugh Edmund Ford*, p.134.

7. *Diu Quidem.*

8. On 26 September, 1900, Edmund Ford was elected the first Abbot of Downside Abbey.

9. *Religious Ordo.*

10. Ibid.

11. *The Weekly Register*, 15 July 1899.

12. Ibid.

13. *The Weekly Register*, 22 July 1899.

14. Ibid.

15. *The Weekly Register*, 29 July 1899.

16. Ibid.

17. *The Weekly Register*, 5 August 1899.

18. *The Catholic Times and Catholic Opinion*, 21 July 1899.

19. Ibid.

20. Ibid., 4 August 1899.

21. Ibid.

22. Ibid., 25 August 1899.

23. Ibid.

24. *The Weekly Register*, 5 August 1899.

25. Ibid.

26. See pp.15.

27. *The Weekly Register*, 22 July 1899.

28. Ibid., 29 July 1899.

29. *Minutes of the Cathedral Chapter of Westminster 31 January 1878 to 7 November 1899*, 4 July 1899.

30. Ibid.

31. Taunton, according to the *Catholic Directory*, 1899, was on sick leave when he wrote this pamphlet. He died in 1907. See *The Tablet*, 18 May 1907, for his obituary.

32. E. L. Taunton, *A Letter to His Eminence Herbert Cardinal Vaughan Archbishop of Westminster on the Work of the Clergy at the Westminster Cathedral* (Exeter: Western Times Office, 1899), p.5.

33. Ibid., p.6.

34. Ibid.

35. Ibid., p.7.

36. Ibid., p.8.

37. Ibid., p.10.

38. Ibid.

39. Vaughan to Delatte, June 1899, Delatte Papers.

40. Cabrol to Delatte, 25 July 1899, Delatte Papers

41. Ibid

42. Cabrol to Vaughan, 4 August 1899, Vaughan Papers, Archbishop's House.

43. Ibid.

44. Vaughan to Cabrol, 3 August 1899, Delatte Papers.

45. Ibid.

46. Cabrol to Delatte, 5 August 1899, Delatte Papers.

47. Ibid.

48. Cabrol to Delatte, 28 August 1899, Delatte Papers.

5. Cardinal Vaughan, the Benedictines and The French Monks.

1. See pp.84ff.

2. Vaughan to Gasquet, 27 November 1900, Gasquet Papers, Downside Abbey Archives, Downside Abbey, Somerset.

3. 'Memorandum As To The Question of Serving Westminster Cathedral,' Gasquet Papers, p.1.

4. Ibid., p.2.

5. Ibid.

6. Delatte to Vaughan, 11 June 1899, Vaughan Papers, Archbishop's House.

7. A. Gasquet, 'Memorandum,' Gasquet Papers, p.2.

8. Ibid.

9. *The Tablet*, 6 October 1900.

10. Ibid.

11. *The Tablet*, 10 November 1900.

12. Ibid.

13. Vaughan to Gasquet, 24 December 1900, Gasquet Papers.

14. Ibid.

15. E. E. Reynolds, *The Roman Catholic Church in England and Wales* (Wheathampstead: Anthony Clarke, 1973), p.353.

16. Vaughan to Gasquet, 24 December 1900, Vaughan Papers, Archbishop's House.

17. Ibid., p.2.

18. Ibid., p.3.

19. Ibid., p.4.

20. Ibid.

21. J. G. Snead-Cox, The Life of Cardinal Vaughan vol. 2, p.356.

22. A. Gasquet, 'Notes,' December 1900, Gasquet Papers.

23. Ibid., p.2.

24. Ibid.

25. *The Tablet*, 2 December 1899.

26. Ibid.

27. Gilbert to Delatte, 21 January 1900, Delatte Papers.

28. Ibid.

29. Delatte to Cabrol, 29 October 1900, Delatte Papers.

30. St. Paul's, Wisques, was founded from Solesmes in 1889 and became a conventual priory in 1895.

31. Delatte to Cabrol, 29 October 1900, Delatte Papers.

32. Gilbert to Delatte, 23 January 1901, Delatte Papers.

33. Gilbert to Delatte, 24 February 1901, Delatte Papers.

6. The Abbot and the Archbishop

1. Gasquet to Vaughan, 13 February 1900, Gasquet Papers.

2. Ibid., p.2.

3. Ibid.

4. Gasquet to Vaughan, 17 February 1901, Vaughan Papers, Archbishop's House.

5. Ibid., p.2.

6. Ibid., p.3.

7. Ibid., p.4.

8. Ibid., p.5.

9. Ibid., p.6.

10. Ibid., p.9.

11. Ibid., p.10-11.

12. Ibid., p.14.

13. Ibid., p.15.

14. Ibid.

15. J. G. Snead-Cox, *The Life of Cardinal Vaughan* vol. 2, p.357.

16. Vaughan to Gasquet, 3 March 1901, Vaughan Papers, Archbishop's House.

17. A. Gasquet, 'Notes of Reply to Card. Vaughan of March 3,' Gasquet Papers.

18. J. G. Snead-Cox, ibid., vol.2, p.357.

19. Cabrol to Vaughan, 17 March 1901, Vaughan Papers, Archbishop's House.

20. J. G. Snead-Cox, ibid., vol. 2, p.357.

21. The Metropolitan Chapter was erected on 19 June 1852. In 1901 the following were members: Provost, Right Rev. Mgr. Michael Barry, V. G. Canons: Right Rev. Mgr. W. A. Johnson, D. D. (Penitentiary); Very Rev. Cornelius J. Keens; Right Revv. Mgr. James Moyes, D. D. (Theologian), Mgr. Patrick Fenton; Very Revv. Leopold Pycke, Reginald Tuke, William L. Gildea, D. D., Edmund Surmont, D. D., Alfred White.

22. *Minutes of the Cathedral Chapter 1899 to 1946*, vol. 5, 23 April 1901.

23. *Synod of Westminster*, XXXII-XLI, 1893-1902, Archbishop's House, p.101.

24. *The Tablet*, 15 June 1901.

25. J. G. Snead-Cox, ibid., vol. 2, p.360.

26. G. Wheeler, 'The Archdiocese of Westminster,' in G. A. Beck, ed., *The English Catholics 1850-1950*, p.170.

27. *Minutes of the Cathedral Chapter of Westminster 1899 to 1946*, 23 April 1901.

28. Dolan to Ford, 12 October 1899, Dolan Papers, Ealing Abbey Archives.

29. Quoted in S. Leslie, *Cardinal Gasquet: A Memoir*, p.198.

30. B. Hicks, *Hugh Edmund Ford*, pp.73-74. The Benedictines from Downside Abbey, however, did not leave London, but remained in Ealing. The parish grew, and in 1902, a school was started. In 1916, the foundation became a dependent priory, in 1947 an independent priory, and in 1955 it was raised to the rank and dignity of an abbey.

7. Cathedral Resplendent: the Fulfilment of the Dream.

1. Quoted in A. McCormack, *Cardinal Vaughan*, p.296.

2. Ibid.

3. *The Universe*, 19 March 1976.

4. *The Universe*, 18 July 1980.

BIBLIOGRAPHY

A. Manuscript Collections

Delatte Papers, Solesmes Abbey Archives, Solesmes, France.

Dolan Papers, Ealing Abbey Archives, Ealing, London.

Farnborough Abbey Archives (photographs), Farnborough.

Ford Papers, Ealing Abbey Archives, Ealing, London.

Ford Papers, Downside Abbey Archives, Downside, Bath.

Gasquet Papers, Downside Abbey Archives, Downside, Bath.

Minutes of the Cathedral, Chapter of Westminster 1899-1946, St. Mary's Presbytery, East Finchley, London.

Vaughan Papers, Archdiocese of Westminster Archives, London.

Vaughan Papers (photographs), St. Joseph Missionary Society, Mill Hill, London.

B. Newspapers and Periodicals

Downside Review.

The Catholic Times and Catholic Opinion.

The Priorian.

The Universe.

The Tablet.

The Times.

The Weekly Register.

C. Reference Works

Catholic Directory.

Dictionary of National Biography.

New Catholic Encyclopedia.

The Oxford Dictionary of the Christian Church.

D. Printed Works

A Mill Hill Father: *Remembered in Blessing: The Courtfield Story*, London, 1969. This short work tells the history of the Vaughan family.

Anson, Peter: *Underground Catholicism in Scotland*, Montrose, 1970. Anson's history of the post-Reformation Roman Catholic Church in Scotland ends with the restoration of the hierarchy in 1878. The author's eye for detail is very good.

Aveling, JCH: *The Handle and the Axe: The Catholic Recusants in England From Reformation to Emancipation*, London, 1976. After a fine introduction, the author explores Catholic history in terms of growth and change.

Beck, George Andrew, (ed): *The English Catholics 1850-1950*, London, 1950. Written to commemorate the hundredth anniversary of the re-establishment of the hierarchy, this work contains essays by scholars on all aspects of Catholic life in England. Articles by Hughes, Gwynn, Matthew, and Cruise deserve attention.

Bossy, John: *The English Catholic Community 1570-1850*, London, 1975. Described as 'a feat of historical sociology,' Bossy's work is the classic examination of English Roman Catholicism from the reign of Elizabeth to the restoration of the hierarchy. This work is essential for an understanding of English Catholicism.

Chadwick, Owen: *The Reformation*, Harmondsworth, 1972. A general history of the Reformation, Chadwick tells the story of the reforming movements of the sixteenth century in England and on the Continent.

—, *The Victorian Church*, Part I and II, London, 1970 A masterpiece of historical research and writing, Chadwick studies the history and developments of religion in Victorian England. His treatment of Roman Catholicism is splendid.

Cragg, Gerald: *The Church and the Age of Reason 1648-1789*, Harmondsworth, 1970. A volume on the Pelican History of the Church. This book is a general survey of church history during the Enlightenment.

Crichton, JD (ed): *English Catholic Worship: Liturgical Renewal in England since 1900*, London, 1979. A series of articles dealing with liturgical renewal, this book skillfully blends history, theology, and liturgy, and the result is an important book for the study of twentieth century Catholicism.

Dickins, AG: *The English Reformation*, London, 1964. Dickens' scholarship and expertise is well recognized. The author's other numerous works on the Reformation should also be consulted.

De L'Hopital, Winefride: *Westminster Cathedral and its Architect*, 2 vols., London, 1919. This book explores the background and the actual building of Westminster Cathedral. The portrait of the architect, Bentley, is good, and the fine collection of photographs adds life to the story of the cathedral.

Green, Bernard: *The English Benedictine Congregation*, London, 1980. This short pamphlet is a popular history of the EBC and a good introduction to Benedictine life in England.

Gwynn, Denis: *The Second Spring, 1818-1852, A Study of the Catholic Revival in England*, London, 1942. Written nearly forty years ago, Gwynn's work still sheds light on the history of early nineteenth century English Roman Catholicism.

Hicks, Bruno: *Hugh Edmund Ford*, London, 1947. A short biography of Ford, this book contains valuable information on Downside's first abbot. The chapter on the 'Constitutional Crisis' gives one a better understanding of this troubled and confused period.

Holmes, J Derek: *More Roman Than Rome: English Catholicism in the Nineteenth Century*, London, 1978. A history of Victorian Roman Catholicism, Holmes discusses the developments within Catholicism in terms of the influence of ultramontanism. He also emphasizes the roles of the Archbishops of Westminster. The author's discussion on Vatican I and infallibility are superior.

Jedin, Hubert (ed): *History of the Church: Reformation and Counter Reformation*, London, 1980.

—, *History of the Church: The Church in the Age of Absolutism and Enlightenment*, London, 1981.

—, *History of the Church: The Church Between Revolution and Restoration*, London, 1981.

—, *History of the Church: The Church in the Age of Liberalism*, London, 1981.

—, *History of the Church: The Church in the Industrial Age*, London, 1981. Edited by Hubert Jedin, these volumes deal with all aspects of European church history. The articles are well-documented, and each volume contains an excellent bibliography.

Jungmann, J A: *Public Worship*, London, 1957. A general history of the rites and liturgies of Roman Catholicism.

Knowles, David: *Cardinal Gasquet as an Historian*, London, 1957. The subject for the 1956 Creighton Lecture in History, Gasquet's contributions to historical research are discussed by David Knowles. the author is critical of Gasquet's methodology and interpretations.

—, *The Monastic Order in England*, Cambridge, 1940.

—, *The Religious Orders in England*, 3 vols., Cambridge, 1950, 1955, 1959. The works of Dom David Knowles are essential for any understanding of early monastic history in England.

Koenker, Ernest: *The Liturgical Renaissance in the Roman Catholic Church*, Chicago, 1954. Written prior to Vatican II, this book gives an adequate history of the development of Roman Catholic liturgy. The author rightly devotes some space to the importance of Solesmes.

Leslie, Shane: *Cardinal Gasquet*, London, 1953. A memoir. 'This biography covers certain periods and the most remarkable seams in a busy and vivid career.' Leslie emphasizes the Cardinal's fight for the Allied cause in Rome during the Great War. Long abstracts from primary sources help to bring the personality of Gasquet to life.

—, *Henry Edward Manning, His Life and Labours*, London, 1921. A biography of Manning, Leslie's use of Manning's correspondence helps one to understand the life of this convert from Anglicanism who became Archbishop of Westminster.

Lunn, David: *The English Benedictines 1540-1688*, London, 1980. 'This book is about change and continuity in English Benedictine monasticism during the transitional period between medieval and modern times', according to Dr. Lunn. Well-documented and researched, the book narrates the story of struggles of English Benedictines in a lively and exciting manner.

McClelland, Vincent A: *Cardinal Manning, His Public Life and Influence 1865-1892*, London, 1962. A good biography of Manning. The author emphasizes his negative attitude toward the proposed Westminster Cathedral. The bibliography can help others who want to pursue a study of Manning's career.

McCormack, Arthur: *Cardinal Vaughan*, London, 1966. Written by a member of St. Joseph's Missionary Society, Mill Hill, McCormack had access to sources unavailable to Snead-Cox, the first biographer of Cardinal Vaughan.

Matthew, David: *Catholicism in England 1535-1935. Portrait of a Minority: Its Culture and Tradition*, London, 1936. According to the foreward, 'this book is intended as a sketch of the contributions of Catholics to English life, a brief impression of the influence of individuals and Catholic groups upon the history of England.'

Norman, Edward: *Anti-Catholicism in Victorian England*, London, 1967. This book is a collection of documents and essays dealing with anti-Catholic prejudices in nineteenth century England. Two articles, 'Anti-Catholic Tradition' and 'Papal Aggression', are excellent.

—, *Roman Catholicism in England From the Elizabethan Settlement to the Second Vatican Council*, Oxford, 1985. This essay deals with the fortunes of Roman Catholicism, a 'religious minority', and points out several continuities in Catholicism's troubled history. Norman's gift of synthesis appears throughout the book.

—, *The English Catholic Church in the Nineteenth Century*, Oxford, 1984. In the most recent history of Victorian Roman Catholicism, the author emphasizes the contributions of great men and instructions, but ignores the recent findings of social history.

Powicke, Maurice: *The Reformation in England*, London, 1973. Originally published in 1941, this short book is an outstanding introduction to the English Reformation.

Purcell, Edmund Sheridan: *Life of Cardinal Manning*, 2 vols., London,1896. The classic, although not totally objective, biography of Cardinal Manning.

Raynolds, E E: *The Roman Catholic Church in England and Wales: A Short History*, Wheathampstead, 1973. This history of Catholicism is meant for the general reader interested in ecclesiastical history. It begins with the arrival of St Augustine and ends in the 1940's.

Snead-Cox, J G: *The Life of Cardinal Vaughan*, 2 vols., London, 1910. The first biography of Vaughan, different from that which portrayed him as aloof and insensitive. Lengthy quotations from Vaughan's papers form the backbone of this book. Snead-Cox's presentation of the story behind the construction of Westminster Cathedral is adequate.

Taunton, E L: *A Letter to His Eminence Herbert Cardinal Vaughan on the Work of the Clergy at the Westminster Cathedral*, Exeter, 1899. A short work written in defense of the rights of the secular clergy and their claims to be responsible for the liturgy at Westminster Cathedral.

The British Library: *The Benedictines in Britain*, London, 1980. This book is a series of essays which commemorated the fifteen-hundredth anniversary of the birth of St. Benedict. The articles are geared for the general public. The illustrations and pictures are outstanding.

Vidler, Alec: *The Church in the Age of Revolution*, Harmondsworth, 1972. Vidler adroitly traces the history of Christianity from the outbreak of the French Revolution to the twentieth century. The sections on Scotland are excellent.

Ward, Bernard: *The Eve of Catholic Emancipation 1803-1829*, 3 vols., London, 1911, 1912. A traditional history of the period, Ward sees Emancipation as the critical phase in the development of English Roman Catholicism.

INDEX OF SUBJECTS AND PLACES

INDEX OF PERSONAL NAMES